Penguin

# YOUR
# CHILDREN'S
# DREAMS

Joan Hanger is an expert throughout Australasia on dream analysis, yet she originally learned about dreams by discussing them with her children over the kitchen table! She then went on to study at the C.G. Jung Institute in Zurich, Switzerland, and now talks dreams with the world through regular national television appearances in Australia, and via BBC in London and CNN in the United States. Joan is also the author of *In Your Dreams*, *Wake Up to Your Dreams* and *The Little Book of Dreams*.

*I wish to dedicate this book to my children
Catherine, Gabrielle, Brigitte and Damien,
and to my baby grandchildren
Olivia and Eloïse.*

*Also, I would like to thank the many
children and friends who became involved
with the idea of this book, and who kindly
sent me their dreams. In particular I would
like to thank Annabelle Quist, Hannah Cox,
Sophie and Georgina Jarvis, Leonie and
Graham Toole at the Kincumber Kids Factory,
and Wayne Stubbs.*

# YOUR CHILDREN'S DREAMS

Understanding what your children's
dreams *really* mean

*Joan Hanger*

with *Catherine Hanger*

PENGUIN BOOKS

Penguin Books Australia Ltd
487 Maroondah Highway, PO Box 257
Ringwood, Victoria 3134, Australia
Penguin Books Ltd
Harmondsworth, Middlesex, England
Penguin Putnam Inc.
375 Hudson Street, New York, New York 10014, USA
Penguin Books Canada Limited
10 Alcorn Avenue, Toronto, Ontario, Canada M4V 3B2
Penguin Books (NZ) Ltd
Cnr Rosedale and Airborne Roads, Albany, Auckland, New Zealand
Penguin Books (South Africa) (Pty) Ltd
4 Pallinghurst Road, Parktown 2193, South Africa

First published by Penguin Books Australia Ltd 1998

10 9 8 7 6 5 4 3 2 1

Design by Marina Messiha, Penguin Design Studio
Typeset in 10½/15pt Berkeley Medium by Post Pre-press Group
   Brisbane, Queensland
Printed and bound in Australia by Australian Print Group
   Maryborough, Victoria

National Library of Australia
Cataloguing-in-Publication data:

Hanger, Joan.

   Your children's dreams : understanding what your children's
   dreams really mean.

   Includes index.
   ISBN 0 14 026590 2.

   1. Children's dreams. 2. Dream interpretation. I. Hanger, Catherine. II. Title.

154.634

# CONTENTS

**KENSINGTON PALACE**

We dream when we are asleep; we dream when we are awake. The latter is usually a vision of happiness and hope, but it is the night-time fantasies of the unconscious mind which are not so easy to translate and which therefore lead us to wonder just how much the goals and aspirations of our waking hours are influenced by them.

The interpretation of her own children's dreams has prompted Joan Hanger to write about her belief that the fears and fantasies expressed in a child's dreams can describe the present and point the way to the future.

As a mother, I know personally how important it is to listen to and evaluate a child's hopes, desires and fears, and dreams provide a window on his or her innermost thoughts.

It is the dream of Barnardos Australia to transform the misery and despair of the children to whom they are committed into happiness and optimism. So it is my great hope that the proceeds from this book will help young people to achieve their dreams of a better future and inspire them, in turn, to pass on that ideal. There is such a need for us all to show by our confidence, compassion, dedication and generosity that the dream of a better world for children can become closer to reality.

Diana

Diana, Princess of Wales
July 1996

# INTRODUCTION

*Your Children's Dreams* is a book for parents. It is designed to be simple without being simplistic, informative without being pedantic, instructive without being rigid. I hope it will give you a deep understanding of children's dreams and how they work, and a broader understanding of the nature of dreams in general.

The first ideas for this book were laid down when I was putting together another book, *Wake Up to Your Dreams*, over two years ago. In fact, a book on children's dreams had been in the back of my mind for some time, due to the great number of letters and wonderful drawings I had been receiving from children for many years. While children have fewer verbal skills than adults, I found their dream stories vivid and interesting, and sometimes disturbing. Their stories gave me insight into little minds that were beginning to comprehend the world and how it worked. Their drawings were often painstakingly detailed, and many of them were startlingly graphic.

It struck me then that dreams were an important indication of children's state of mind and how they coped with the various stages of their development. It also struck me that, because children are too young to have developed the defences and prejudices of adults, they took their dreams very seriously indeed.

To children, dreams are like play. By this, I do not mean that dreams are frivolous, however, because children's play is definitely not frivolous. Play is a crucial behavioural mechanism of childhood used by children to work out scenarios that are current in their lives. These scenarios include their relationships, their worries, their desires, their fantasies and their fears. Play can, of course, be enormous fun, and it is always something of a relief for children to be able to express themselves in this way. Play is largely unconscious for children. It is something that they do to let off steam in all the areas of their life that they are exploring or that are having an impact on them in some way. For discerning adults, children's play can be extremely revealing in terms of how they are dealing with the inevitable conflicts and challenges that arise in the course of their development. Child psychologists often observe a child at play in a constructed setting to deepen their understanding of particular problems or issues that the child may have.

Like play, dreams can also be fun and tremendously exciting for children, and they are marvellous tools for expanding creativity. Dreams are unconscious ways in which children work out their concerns, although they have special components that play does not: dreams happen only in children's minds and do not have any sense of predetermined *volition* because they happen when children are asleep. For this reason, dreams are sometimes quite disturbing for children, and some may feel helpless in the face of a bad dream or nightmare. Dreams are also elusive because they do not stick to the normal waking parameters of time, place and linear thought.

Children are also very much subject to the psychic environment in which they find themselves. The environment will inexorably shape the child's personality. For instance, children who grow up in a household where dreams are dismissed, misunderstood or simply not discussed will not know how to use one of the most important tools of their unconscious mind.

Such a loss would be a shame. Firstly, children will lose touch with a richly creative part of themselves. Secondly, they will not develop the skills that come about when they are encouraged to examine and interpret their dreams, and integrate them into their concept of self and behaviour. Thirdly, while children will continue to dream – because dreams are an activity of each and every human mind – those who are without some interpretive skills may remain uncomprehending. Consequently, they may be plagued by dreams that are trying to tell them something, but they are without the keys to understanding. Parental guidance in the area of children's dreams is crucial, as it is in every area of their lives.

Many adults themselves seem to have lost touch with their creative unconscious. The effect such a loss has on their dreams is considerable: many are disturbed by dreams of which they can make neither head nor tail, but which they know are somehow significant to their lives. These dreams are like bad habits that press in on the dreamer until steps are taken to understand and realign their psyche. If children grow up without knowing how to deal with their dreams they will not know how to deal with a fundamental part of themselves, which will almost certainly bother them at a later stage.

In the course of my work, I have received many letters from concerned parents and their children, and drawings by children, on their dreams. Many parents wanted some guidance to their children's inner world of dreams that was related to the accepted milestones of childhood development, but found there was little material to which they could refer.

I hope this book goes some way towards meeting those needs.

In Chapters 1 and 2, I offer a discussion of the basic aspects of dreams and how they reveal themselves with special reference to children. I examine broadly some aspects of child development that are crucial to understanding how children see their dreams, and how they operate within the context of their age and environment.

Chapter 3 deals specifically with nightmares and night terrors, which can be extremely distressing for children and are often the first indication to parents that their child is dreaming. Parents need to develop some basic skills to reassure their distressed child, and to help him or her work through the often very 'normal' problems that are part of childhood which may be expressed in bad dreams. I also look at positive action parents can use and teach to their children.

In Chapter 4, I examine some common dream themes and what they might mean. Chapter 5 contains practical measures that parents can use to encourage the discussion and interpretation of dreams with their children. Chapter 6 takes a brief look at issues such as health and the media, which can have a strong effect on children's dreams in general.

It is my hope that this book will enable you, the parent, to assist your children by giving you a greater understanding of the nature of dreams and what they indicate in the context of normal childhood development. Bear in mind that so-called 'normal' development is a concept that works on the principle of averages. Every child is unique and will demonstrate special aptitudes, likes and dislikes, and ways of coping and behaving that could – indeed should – deviate to some extent from the mean.

To finish, a 'dream story' that goes with this book, one that is related to the foreword, written by the late Diana, Princess of Wales.

While I was putting together my thoughts and

mulling over the structure for *Your Children's Dreams*, I watched a television programme on Diana's patronage of children's charities. A bright light shone! I contacted Barnardos, one of the charities she worked with at the time, and with their assent, wrote to her to request her involvement.

Her reply was prompt and positive. Yes, she was very interested in children's dreams, having had many discussions about dreams with children and with her two sons, William and Harry; and yes, she would love to meet me to discuss the proposal for the book.

I met with Diana at her home in Kensington Palace in London in 1996. We discussed dreams, her sons, her hopes for their

Diana encouraged her sons, William and Harry, to talk with her about their dreams.

future, my children, my hopes for the book and many other things. I found her delightful – open, intuitive, helpful and warm. It seemed extraordinary to be swapping mundane details of our lives over a cup of tea, and it gave me a strong sense of the ordinary human side to this woman whose life had become so avidly devoured in the pages of publications worldwide. Diana was eager to lend her support to *Your Children's*

*Dreams*, and keen to write a foreword to the book. She was well aware that she could help to raise the profile of the subject and to focus attention on Barnardos and the importance of children's welfare.

Diana was as good as her word.

Reams have been written and said about Diana. For me, she was a person who genuinely and deeply cared about children. She knew that her position would be invaluable in attracting public attention to any area she felt to be worthwhile. She realised the fragility and preciousness of children's minds, and she was aware that a healthy adult psyche grew from a solid base in childhood. Diana was very interested in dreams and discussed them with great sensitivity. I hope she would have enjoyed reading this book.

# DREAMS AND CHILDREN

It is an unfortunate fact of parenting that your first contact with children's dreams is likely to be in the middle of the night when your child awakes from a nightmare. You will have to comfort the tearful bundle and listen, if he or she is old enough to recount the dreadful events. You will have to reassure your child that it is safe to go to sleep again, and probably stay until he or she does. You may have to weather intermittent night awakenings due to children's nightmares, which, like teething, are a disagreeable but typical feature of the nocturnal life of a normal, developing child.

Nightmares are dreams that are unpleasant enough to break through the surface of sleep, forcing a child to wake. But nightmares are really just the tip of the iceberg. Rest assured that the average child has a night life dense with all sorts of dreams, good and bad, most of which remain submerged in sleep.

Unlike the purely physical process of teething, dreams are a crucial part of the ongoing evolution of your child's psyche. Any parent who is concerned about their child's well-being will also be concerned about the nature of their child's dreams because dreams are one of the most important ways in which the developing identities of children are expressed.

We now know that all the indicators of the dreaming state are present *in utero*: the developing foetus shows dream-like activity from its third trimester. Most parents have watched in wonder as their newborn child dreams, with whimpers and twitches and cries. The mind of a child, like its body, is fully formed at birth; immature but powerfully programmed to grow along predetermined pathways to adulthood. Like the body, the mind can be nurtured or it can be stunted in its growth. As you watch for the physical signs of a thriving child, so you should watch for signs that he or she is mentally content. Dreams are one of the most important signals of a child's state of mind.

The business of growing up is demanding. All children have to cope with unavoidable crises: separation from the mother; sibling rivalry; having to learn to delay gratification; restraining powerful aggressive urges; developing a sense of a place in the world; succeeding at school and being with friends. And that is within a perfectly standard upbringing at any time, anywhere in the world. Add to these pressures those of divorce, blended families, poverty and abuse, for example, and the life of a child begins to look complicated indeed.

Nightmares, while 'normal', are indicators of the

anxieties that affect your children. On the one hand, these anxieties may be simply healthy responses to the milestones of daily life. On the other, they may indicate extraordinary stresses taking their toll on an immature and fragile identity.

That first distressing nightmare can be productive, however. Firstly, it alerts you to things that may be troubling your child in his or her daily life. Secondly, it can be made a starting point for discussion and encouragement: as you will discover, it is possible for children to work out difficulties that are being expressed in a dream within the dream itself. Once a child starts to discuss the nightmare, the trouble, and its possible resolution, he or she is also likely to tell you all sorts of other important things about this dream life, from joyful experiences of flying and confident self-portrayals as a hero or warrior to visitations from magical characters that may have correlations in the child's waking life. Dreams can open up a marvellous opportunity for dialogue with your children, and allow you to monitor – and nurture – their growing self-esteem, strength of character and imagination.

## What Are Dreams and What Do They Mean?

Put simply, dreams are symbolic images created in our unconscious while we are asleep to feed messages to our waking mind.

There are many schools of thought on why we dream, but it was two psychologists, Sigmund Freud and Carl Jung, who revolutionised the way in which we now perceive the mind to work.

Freud (1856–1939) is known as the father of modern psychology. He developed a treatment called psychoanalysis which is now widely used to treat mental and personality disorders and problems. Psychoanalysis works by examining the underlying unconscious motivations in an effort to make them conscious, and thus able to be assimilated into the individual's personality, behaviour and perception. Freud's view was that all behaviour is caused, therefore strange or inappropriate behaviours are symptoms of an underlying personality defect or unconscious motive.

Freud's views have been widely debated, but his basic findings are still the touchstone of modern psychological theory. *The Interpretation of Dreams*, a book he published in 1900, explained his work with dream therapy and his views on the importance of dreams in the unconscious life of a person. He regarded the dream images as 'manifest content', which screened thoughts that he called 'latent content'. Such thoughts were screened because they were troubling or unacceptable to the dreamer. (This idea is the precursor of Jung's idea of compensation, which will be explained later.) To help his patients identify the latent content, Freud developed a process of word association around the image of the dream. Then he interpreted the dream in light of what came out of the word associations, and identified and treated the unconscious problems underpinning the dream.

Freud maintained that we dream to fulfil our deepest wishes. On the topic of unpleasant dreams, he said that they expressed a desire, but are unpleasant because the conscious mind finds the desire objectionable or alarming, and thus represses it.

Carl Jung (1875–1961) worked with Freud but broke away because he disagreed with some of his theories, although he always generously acknowledged his debt to Freud. Jung made a life-long study of dreams, and his work is integral to the history of dream therapy, and the basis of what we know today on the subject.

Jung said that dreams expressed the current state of the dreamer's unconscious. He pointed out that dream images are symbolic and complex, but that each dream symbol is uniquely created by the dreamer and resonates with meaning specifically for that person. So, it is essential for the dreamer to learn to examine the layers of meaning to arrive at the message. It is this process – exploring the dream and working with it towards an understanding of the particular and specific message – that we will examine in this book.

In Jung's view, a dream was not necessarily only about wish-fulfilment, and he did not hold to Freud's idea of manifest and latent content. For him, the dream was itself the context, and he preferred to work with the patient on the symbols that were presented, using his knowledge to help the patient come to the meaning of the dream. According to Jung, 'the whole dream work is essentially subjective, and a dream is the theatre in which the dreamer is himself the scene, the player, the prompter, the producer, the author, the public, and the critic' (C.G. Jung, *Dreams*, page 52).

Jung's exploration of the unconscious mind took him into the study of mythology, anthropology, religion and art. He connected the work of psychology to all of these areas. He also developed the idea of archetypes, which is essential in the understanding of dream content.

## The Unconscious

In our conscious mind, we perceive through our senses and we filter all that information through the faculty of reason. But every conscious event has an unconscious component. For example, you may have sat through a meeting at work, and only later in the day be bothered by the demeanour of one of the participants, which may lead you to a totally different perspective on what was said. This is your unconscious working things through at a different level. Or, you may remember, in the middle of the night, where you have put something you thought you had lost. Or, you may suddenly solve a problem, seemingly by intuition. All of these situations are examples of the unconscious mind interrelating with your conscious, rational thought processes.

Dreams are part of the process of revision that the unconscious does on conscious events. This is why dreamers can be so affected by their dreams – the dreams mirror, in a profound but exaggerated way, their major concerns. Often the mirror is complex and shifting, and shows the other side, perhaps a side that the dreamer has not admitted to or seen in a situation. They may throw up seemingly absurd scenarios, like those that Alice encountered in Wonderland and Looking Glass Land. Dreams let us know when we are ambivalent, struggling or positive.

Children are born unconscious of themselves. Because of their inability to separate inner from outer realities, dreams can be extremely unsettling for children, especially when the dreams are borne of anxiety or unresolved conflicts. A major concern of childhood is the drive to consciousness, meaning that children become increasingly conscious of themselves, their place in the family and the world, and their existence as separate beings. Gradually, they separate from the mother and become individuals. They have to learn objectivity and rational thought. This process is marked by the development of what Freud called the *ego*. We will learn more about this process later, in Chapter 2.

With many adults, the unconscious has been driven underground, and life exists entirely in the conscious here and now. Dreams may be dismissed or left unremembered. When adults lose touch with their unconscious, they lose touch with much of what concerns children. This is why many parents are perplexed by their children's anxieties and troubled dreams. It is very important that parents are able to tap into their unconscious and creative or destructive minds so that they can assist their children for whom the unconscious world of dreams can be so disturbing, but also so rewarding.

## Archetypes

Jung developed the concept of archetypes, a concept essential to a deeper understanding of dream processes, and particularly important in understanding the dreams of children. Archetypes are inherited, primordial images that exist as part of the biological apparatus of our unconscious. They are dormant in every child's mind until activated by life events that bring the archetype into a specific focus. For Jung, archetypes are a function of the *collective unconscious*, meaning that there exist in human beings 'certain psychic and behavioural forms which, while achieving unique expression in each individual are, at the same time, universally present in all members of our species'. (Anthony Stevens,

*Archetypes: A Natural History of the Self*, page 14).

For example, the Mother is an archetype. A child's relationship with the Mother figure will determine how this image is experienced. An archetype that Jung called 'the Shadow' is another that is especially important to children. In children's dreams, the Shadow often appears as the threatening stranger or monster.

These two archetypes would have been crucial images to all children from the time of our primitive forbears, because they signal two biological essentials to a child's vulnerable life: fundamental nurturing and the necessity to flee larger, life-threatening beings. While archetypes develop a great deal of symbolic complexity in adult dreams (where they will indicate crucial features of the psychological balance of the dreamer), we can see them operating with startling clarity in the dreams of children. Fears of being devoured, abandoned or drowned, for example, are expressed with brutal directness. While these are symbols, as all dream images are, they are also real-life possibilities to a small child at the mercy of adults and larger elemental forces. So, for children, an archetypal dream expresses human biological heritage as well as the state of the developing Self of the particular child.

## Special Characteristics of Dreams

Our dreams have particular characteristics that make them both powerful and elusive.

Dreams are often difficult to remember because they do not necessarily unfold in a single dimension of time, space and place. They perplex conscious thought processes that work most effectively with a linear, sequential narrative. Also, dreams are full of strange configurations of characters and events that may seem too bizarre to bother with on awakening. In addition, it appears that in REM sleep – the phase of sleep in which we dream most vividly – the brain cells that secrete the chemicals needed to stimulate memory shut down or operate only sluggishly. This is one of the reasons why it is so much easier to re-member a dream when we are woken directly from it.

In the dream state, the rational, critical faculty of our mind is suspended, and we are usually unable to take an objective viewpoint on what is happening to us. Some dreams may be disturbing because we feel helpless. Or we may feel wonderful while experi-encing a wish-fulfilment dream, only to awake with bitter disappointment!

This book will teach you, the parent, to teach yourselves and your children how to change the direction of a dream to achieve a positive outcome. This is called *lucid dreaming*, and it means that some part of the conscious mind remains vigilant during sleep to direct the dream scenario. It is possible to train the mind to do this (see Chapter 5).

Another major characteristic of dreams is their symbolic nature. Symbols are visual representations that stand in for a complex group of ideas, states, feelings or even people, and are often a distillation of many complicated and sometimes ambivalent responses to a situation or feeling. In dreams, they often represent repressed ideas or thoughts that are otherwise inexpressible, either because they are dangerous (from a child's point of view, a dangerous thought would be wanting to kill a newborn sibling out of a sense of jealous rage) or unacceptable (the necessity of separating from the mother, for example). They may also sum up elusive feeling-states of anxiety, or they may indicate great contentment, joy and hope. Generally, they describe in some important image or series of images the deepest feelings of the dreamer.

If we remember for a moment that a dream is a message from the unconscious to the conscious mind, then we will understand why dreams happen in symbolic language. The unconscious is not precise, logical or critical; it is the repository of feelings just as they are. Necessarily, the conscious mind shoves away a great number of these feelings in the back cupboard of the unconscious because they are too difficult or destructive or fantastical to be expressed. Nevertheless they exist. They reappear in dreams, often disguised, since the conscious mind has rejected them in their raw, unadulterated form. Symbols in dreams are evidence of the mind evaluating and processing our deepest feelings and instincts.

There are many important distinctions to be made between the dreams of adults and the dreams of children. Adults filter the world through the faculty of reason. Children do not. For a child, reasoning is not yet a developed function, and is something that happens only with practice and maturity. This leads to a particular relationship to the unconscious which can make the symbolism of children's dreams much closer to reality, and therefore, often more frightening. However, disguise is also a feature of children's dreams, and it is this element that parents need to be aware of.

The reasons for disguise in dreams are threefold. First, our natural tendency to repress whatever is unpleasant or unacceptable in our feelings. Second, a dream is not a conscious, rational thought: it is a symbol or metaphor. Third, a dream will often condense material. So, very 'charged' thoughts will often coalesce (as feelings often do!) and appear in a symbol that may be difficult to decipher at first glance. In this case, the feeling-tone of the symbol and the dream will be crucial. You will learn how to unravel all of these elements later, in Chapter 5.

Another disturbing, and sometimes exciting, feature of dreams is that they do not conform to morality. Morals are a construction of the conscious mind, and the unconscious has no truck with morality. Neither, of course, do children – until they learn the boundaries of the value system in which they are brought up. Morality is often a highly charged area of feeling for adults. A dream may use the metaphor of morality to express something important about the feelings of the dreamer. For an adult, the most obvious example would be an erotic dream. In this case, sex is as likely to be a metaphor as simple wish-fulfilment.

For children, who are driven much more completely by their unconscious, the lines are very blurred. If we take the sibling rivalry example again, a child may dream of joyously murdering his or her newborn brother. This dream does not mean that the child is likely to do so, only that he or she is repressing feelings of rage and jealousy that parents would do well to acknowledge. The child may, of course, in some way truly want to get rid of the new brother or sister – the usurper – and in this sense the dream is a wish-fulfilment, not just a symbol of unbearable feelings. If the child finds the desire very uncomfortable, there may be dreams of losing the brother. This would be more acceptable to the developing sense of conscience and would not incur parental wrath. It would also be more acceptable to the dreamer as it is a symbolic disguise for his or her feelings.

Another feature of dreams is their compensatory function. This means that they are designed to correct imbalances occurring in the conscious life of the dreamer. The imbalances are usually set in place to prevent the outburst of difficult feelings, so it follows that the dream compensations are likely to be disturbing. They are images from the 'back cupboard' that have been assiduously hidden. When the cupboard threatens to burst at the seams, nightmares may occur. Nightmares are an attempt to force the dreamer to acknowledge something. If the offending feeling is not outed and examined, then nightmares will recur. In adults, we also see unresolved feelings inserting themselves into conscious life in the form of neuroses and obsessions.

Children generally do not have the facility of a 'back cupboard' in which to store unacceptable feelings because they do not have fully formed reason and will with which to create such a compartment. So, for a child who is doing his or her best to be 'good' and 'acceptable', the bad feeling may be pretty overwhelming and lead to nightmares and bad dreams. Bear in mind that young children are not yet independent, and any bad feelings that threaten the source of love and attention will seem very dangerous indeed. It is crucial – physically and psychically – for them to be loved and nurtured by their parents.

Dreams are usually connected with the experiences of the preceding day. This experience may not be an event: it may be a preoccupying train of thought or a strong impression. The unconscious latches onto the experience as a medium or mirror through which to convey the message. Adult dreamers also often incorporate memories of long-forgotten events, people or feeling-states in their dreams. These fragments are indicative of a significant symbolic connection to the situation that is being worked on in the dream. Older children may also experience dreams in which early memories are evoked.

## Sleep Rhythms and Dreams

As I mentioned earlier, children begin to dream in the womb, when the foetal brain starts to show signs of a special sort of activity associated with dreaming – REM sleep. REM stands for Rapid Eye Movement, because that is what is observed during this phase of sleep. During REM sleep, images are formed in the brain and 'seen' as dreams. We do not know if foetal REM is visual (it probably is not), but it probably indicates that the brain is rehearsing for the birth and the life of a new person, complete with the capacity to dream. Newborns spend a lot of their sleep time in REM-phase sleep.

Sleep is not a uniform state. The sleeping brain is constantly oscillating in phases and waves. As we fall asleep, we may have sensations of falling, and small, vivid images may float into our minds, called *hypnagogic* dreams. In stage 1 sleep we relax and our heart rate slows. In stage 2 sleep our brain waves change, showing quick bursts of activity. In stage 3 sleep our brains produce long, slow waves; the heart rate drops further, as do body temperature and blood pressure. Stage 4 sleep is known as *delta* sleep, after the brain waves of the same name produced during this cycle. This is very deep sleep, when the sleeper is virtually immobile and almost impossible to rouse. Night terrors happen during this phase, as do sleep-walking and bed-wetting.

After this phase, our brains start to float up again, and we enter the first period of REM sleep. The body, although effectively paralysed, shows signs of activity and tension, the breathing changes and the sleeper may even mutter. This is the first dream cycle.

From this point, the brain cycles through periods of REM followed by periods of more or less deep sleep at 60 to 90-minute intervals. The REM period may last up to 20 minutes, with dreams becoming more complex and colourful towards morning.

## Sexuality and Children's Dreams

Sexual symbolism in dreams should be noted and treated with great delicacy. Implying sexual symbolism is one thing; imposing it is another. As with all areas of dream interpretation, avoid suggesting meaning to your child. Children are sexual and sensual beings, who are naturally and habitually experimenting with their burgeoning sense of gender and what that means (see Chapter 6), but to launch into a Freudian explanation of a child's dream is not advisable. While children will report dreams that seem to have a symbolic sexual content, I think that generally, the only directly sexual connotation of dreams that should be drawn by parents is a purely physical one: during REM sleep, genital arousal is normally observed. I will examine the development of sexual identity of children in more detail in Chapter 2.

I urge that sexual themes in children's dreams be read with care and great neutrality on the parents' part, provided that the dreams do not indicate persistent and worrying themes such as rape, seduction or any other element that suggests your child is being abused or somehow interfered with. For example, if your child is dreaming about graphic sexual acts which are obviously not in keeping with his or her age and understanding, then this is cause for concern. Similarly, if the child is dreaming of aggressive acts directed towards him or her in an obviously sexual manner, then help should be sought.

In the normal course of events, the natural curiosity of children will bring them to you with questions about sex and all its implications, and it is at that point that it should be discussed.

Children also fantasise, but the details of their fantasy are limited to what they can imagine. If children are being fed a diet of lurid television and videos with adult themes, then it is likely that they will reproduce some of these events in their dreams, even if they do not really comprehend the meaning.

## SUMMARY

☼ Dreams are one of the important ways in which children express their emerging identity.

☼ Dreams are often indicators of a child's state of mind at the time.

☼ Nightmares are common to all children and are clues to the anxieties affecting your child. These anxieties can be due to the normal challenges of growing up, or they can point to more serious stresses.

☼ Dreams are symbolic images created in our minds when we are asleep which indicate the current state of the dreamer's unconscious. Each symbolic image is unique to each dreamer, which means that while common images recur throughout history and cultures, they will have special and specific meanings for the individual dreamer. The best person to interpret the dream is the dreamer.

☼ The unconscious interrelates with conscious rational thought processes but revises them in a different way. Dreams are part of our unconscious revision.

☼ Children are born unconscious and gradually develop a conscious, rational mind.

☼ Archetypes are inherited, primordial images that exist in the psyches of all people. They are activated in a child's mind by life events that bring the archetype into specific focus for that child.

☼ The Mother and the Shadow are archetypes with particular relevance to children because from the beginning of time they signal two essentials in a child's life: nurturing and the necessity to flee life-threatening beings.

☼ Because dreams do not unfold in the linear, logical way our waking mind is accustomed to, dreams are often difficult to remember. However, dreams are usually connected with events in real life.

☼ When dreaming, the rational, critical part of our mind is suspended. Dreams are used by the unconscious to compensate for imbalances in the conscious life of the dreamer.

☼ Dreams are symbolic and use disguise to mask unpleasant aspects of our feelings. Neither do they conform to morality.

☼ Dreams occur in REM (Rapid Eye Movement) sleep, which occurs in cycles throughout the night.

☼ Parents should be wary of interpreting sexual symbolism in children's dreams.

# 2

## CHILD DEVELOPMENT
## AND DREAMS

Children's dreams take place in the crucible of a developing personality. The emerging Self forms gradually, punctuated by inherent psychological conflicts that both challenge and stimulate maturity. Every child endures tests that forge character and identity. These crises are an essential part of growing up.

To newborn children, the world is merely an extension of their waving limbs. Within weeks, they learn to differentiate themselves through physical sensations: being carried or put down, feeding, cuddling, feeling hot and cold, being clothed or unclothed. By four months, children will begin to interact socially with family and visitors. They will smile, and watch for their parents' movements. They will start to babble, play with objects, and learn gradually that such objects can come and go, and that they can control the objects' coming and going. Their motor skills will increase. They will start to eat 'solid' food, and even start to refuse it with seeming capriciousness.

The child's development is continuous and relentless, and happens on the physical, psychological and interpersonal levels. Dreams are concerned mainly with the emotional aspect of self-development (although some dreams seem to prefigure or indicate health issues, see Chapter 6). It is the emotional aspect of child development – the development of Self or personality in its broad sense – that will be examined here.

## The Concept of Self

The Self is the whole psyche: the conscious and unconscious parts, the inner and outer sense of being, our self-esteem and individual and unique relationship with the people and the environment around us. Freud spoke of the components of Self in terms of three 'sections': the *id*, the *ego* and the *superego*. These concepts comprise a good system for understanding the various levels on which our minds deal with the world.

The id is the inner subjective self. It does as it feels. It is not bound by rules, conventions or values and it does not reflect. The id is driven by what Freud called the *pleasure principle* to achieve whatever instinctual needs are paramount at the time. A newborn mind is dominated by the id, or in Jung's sense, the unconscious. The id is the foundation on which all Self is built and is the generating force of dreams.

The ego is like the director of the Self. If the personality is well adjusted, the ego is the balancing force, regulating demands of the id and the superego through the power of reason. The ego is motivated by reality. It is the part of us that learns to delay gratification, to solve problems and to exercise our intellect. The ego is objective, and uses the tool of memory to set and achieve aims.

The superego is the value system or morality of a Self. It regulates both the ideals and the conscience of an individual. It also regulates anti-social behaviour (particularly in the areas of sex and aggression) and is the repository of the traditional values handed down by the society in which the individual grows up.

In a harmonious personality, all parts of the Self operate in smooth integration. But that is the ideal. At various times of our lives and under pressure from various stresses, any one of the three parts may dominate. In childhood, it is most certainly the id that holds sway. It is the emergence of the ego and superego – the conscious parts of the Self – that marks the child's struggle to grow up well. In children, as in adults, the purpose of dreams is to indicate disturbances in equilibrium between the forces of id, ego and superego, or, in Jungian terms, the balance between the conscious and unconscious Self.

The process of growth involves conflict. Growth is achieved only through balancing the desire to go forward with the need to preserve the gains already made. This is why you may notice that your child will regress slightly just before or just after an important milestone (first day at school is a good example). Along with uncharacteristic behaviour (tantrums, aggression or bed-wetting, for example), these regressions may be marked with troubling dreams.

## Stages of Emotional Growth

*Trust* is the bedrock of the child's emerging personality. To maintain stability, infants must be sure that the responses to their behaviour are consistent and that their needs are satisfactorily met. When stability and consistency are present, the child will then begin to assume that positive experiences will continue and can be relied upon – that he or she will be nurtured and held, his or her cries will be heard, and hunger will be satisfied.

From this point, children can move out into their environment to explore the *boundaries of control* over themselves and the world. This is the toddler phase, marked by tantrums and power battles, most of which occur at the limit of the boundaries set by adults. During this phase, it is important for parents to maintain a balance between allowing the child's drive for autonomy to flourish, as well as creating realistic boundaries in which to operate. Limits appear to be beneficial to children: they foster trust and prevent the large and complex world from being too overwhelming, besides encouraging children's confidence in their own abilities to master the world. If the child's autonomy is crushed by boundaries that are too narrow or rigid, however, then an all-pervasive sense of shame may invade the fragile personality.

The next step in a child's path is the *phase of invention or initiative*. From the ages of about three to five, children play with imagination and ideas about what sort of person they can be. Inflated fantasy is a feature of this period, and is often displayed through all sorts of creative outlets: drawing, dancing, role-playing. This is probably the best time to start discussing dreams with your child, because dreams are a perfect vehicle for expression of this sort. Dreams, by their very nature, mirror the fantasy/ reality dynamic with which the child is now pre-occupied. It is at this point that the child feels the first pricks of conscience.

This is the phase when over- and under-achievers are formed. The danger for parents now is to misinterpret a child's flights of fancy. Too much inhibition breeds guilt in the child, who may feel that his or her productions and imaginative essays are inadequate or somehow wrongful.

These first steps are critical in children's emotional development, since they determine the children's sense of being able to operate successfully in their environment besides laying down definitions of self that will be tested through the experimentation characteristic of adolescence, when a true sense of identity is determined.

Children learn *competence* during the years between early childhood and adolescence. They are at school, and working through that system to achieve success in defined areas. The characteristic focus of these years is the purposeful accumulation of tangible skills. The development of perseverance, attentiveness, patience and tenacity are the ideal results. Emotionally, a child is slowly separating from the mother during this phase. This inexorable but frightening separation, combined with the necessity to achieve set goals at school, can generate a great deal of anxiety, some of which may be discharged in dreams. In addition, the child is developing interpersonal sophistication through interactions with the family and in the playground. These social demands may also find release in dreams.

## The Development of Language

As children grow up, they will acquire and become adept at certain skills that will be essential to their development. One of the most important of these is language. Language allows children to define their own space conceptually. It gives children a tool with which to describe and define their feelings, and enables them to elucidate their needs clearly. The development of language has obvious significance for children's dream-life, because it allows them to communicate with their parents, with increasing sophistication, about the content of their dreams.

Strong evidence suggests that children dream from the time they are in the womb, but parents can do nothing about dreams that occur in the pre-linguistic phase, because children cannot tell their parents what is happening to them. Language development is a function of the maturation of the central nervous system. This system also controls perception, memory, judgement and the ability to think. All of these attributes are connected to the mastery of language. Memory becomes increasingly important to a child's dream life as he or she matures. Memories will be used symbolically in dreams to indicate specific states of mind.

Children babble until they are about a year old, when the first words may appear. At twelve to fifteen months, two-word 'phrases' may be uttered. At around sixteen to eighteen months, the child may be able to communicate in short sentences. By the time children are two years old, they have a vocabulary of around 300 words. At three years, they have a vocabulary of about 1000 words. Between three and five years, about fifty words per month are added to this base.

## The Development of Objectivity

Another critical development in the life of a child is the gradual separation of inner and outer states, or the separation of the subjective and objective. This development has crucial implications for parents trying to assist their children's understanding of dreams.

Children have difficulty separating dreams from waking life. To do so demands comprehension of objective (outer) and subjective (inner) states. This immaturity gives rise to much anxiety for children and it is essential for parents to comprehend the limitations of their child's mind.

For children to survive in the world, they must learn the difference between what is happening in their mind and what is happening in reality. The mind must be perceived to be separate from the physical world. In Freudian terms, the ego must emerge and separate from the id, and start to regulate conscious thoughts and activities. At first children do not perceive themselves as separate from anything around them. They learn separation through physical sensation. From the first days of life, children are learning to differentiate what is outside, in the external world, and what is inside, in their thoughts and impulses.

Swiss psychologist Jean Piaget described a number of features of magical thinking in early childhood. For example, a child (let's say it's a boy) up to the age of four or five may believe that by going to bed, he causes the sun to disappear. He believes that everyone thinks and desires as he does. He believes that all things are 'alive', even inanimate objects. Later, he comes to think that only moving objects are alive. It is not until the child is around ten that he understands that only animals and plants are alive in the same way as he is.

Up until about the age of ten, this child thinks that words, pictures, dreams, objects and people are equally 'real'; that is, he does not differentiate between the representation and the thing itself. Piaget described the process of objectifying the internal world of dreams in three stages:

> 1. Up to the age of three or four, children do not distinguish between dreams and waking life. They may wake up from a nightmare, for example, and believe the terrible witch is still under the bed. Parental attempts at reassurance that 'it was only a nasty dream' may be ineffective. Only the practical demonstration that there is indeed nothing under the bed will bring relative peace of mind.
> 2. Between four and six they begin to distinguish between dreamt events and outer events, but they still have difficulty in understanding that what is dreamt is purely internal and not related to external reality.
> 3. Between five and eight they are able to comprehend that dreams are exclusively internal phenomena; and the first lucid dreams often occur at this stage. (Anthony Stevens, *Private Myths, Dreams and Dreaming*, pages 257–58.)

## Childhood Anxiety

Anxiety is the by-product of the tough business of growing up, and unfortunately is a feeling that characterises all stages of the development of children. It is part of the human condition, a feeling that accompanies human existence. Anxiety is a continuum of feeling that goes from vigilant wariness to bowel-melting fear. It is also the emotion that gives rise to the greater number of dreams. Just as dreams will reflect the typical anxieties of a child on his or her developmental pathway, so too will they reflect the child's hopes and desires.

A child that is overloaded with anxiety may be prevented from moving confidently onto the next stage of development. He or she may be prevented from learning, from reaching out, from pursuing relationships and from constructive, enriching play.

Many factors influence children's ability to successfully cope with crises, but one thing is sure: every child suffers anxiety at the various critical points that herald changes in his or her perception of self and the surrounding environment. Change causes anxiety, and childhood is full of change. Some anxiety is useful: it alerts a child to danger and puts him or her psychologically and physiologically in a state to deal with what may be a very real threat. This is called the 'fight or flight' instinct, meaning that the whole being is prepared to run away or to defend itself.

As I noted in Chapter 1, children are subject to archetypal fear in a more direct way than adults. These fears are pictured graphically in dreams. Similarly, they are subject to daily worries as they cope with the changing demands of growing up. Essentially anxiety is unavoidable for children because of their helplessness. Indeed, specific fears and anxieties have been used by psychologists to mark out the developmental trends of childhood. The fear of strangers that is typically observed in children of about six to eight months is a good example.

Generally speaking, parents can rest assured that anxiety is normally observed in children and reflected in their dreams. Sensitive parental reassurance of the child is the ideal treatment. Unpleasant dreams and nightmares only need become cause for real concern if the child begins to lose sleep through fear, or if the nightmares are recurring and seriously disruptive. In these cases, parents would be wise to seek professional guidance. We will discuss specific subjects of anxiety dreams and their content in Chapter 3.

Children are dependent on adults for their survival, so it is essential that adults – namely, the parents – provide for them a stable, nurturing environment where they can experiment with their growing Self in physical and emotional safety.

## Separation and Independence

The development of the Self requires growing independence from parents. This can cause great ambivalence in children. On the one hand, they desire to set off on their own pathways – this may manifest as a refusal of food, attempts to toddle into forbidden zones, getting lost at the supermarket, or tantrums – while on the other, they continue to need the presence and guidance of their parents.

Parents will notice that essays into independent thought and action are accompanied by some anxiety. Being naughty attracts the wrath of Mother, yet it is unhealthy for children to remain passive when all their impulses are urging them to explore boundaries. Conversely, the anger of a parent from a child's point of view can be terrifying because it threatens the very basis of his or her existence. So a child is caught in a cleft stick of anxiety. If the anxiety becomes over-whelming, bad dreams may result.

---

*Recently, I had a dream that I was in a detention centre for girls where I wasn't allowed to go on a day trip. The next day, my mother, my stepfather and I went to the psychologist where they called me by my stepfather's surname then gave me a new uniform with my sister's name on it. Then I realised I was really my sister! What does this mean? (Sam, 12)*

There is an identity crisis here! The crisis is happening in gender, family and sibling terms. The detention centre is an interesting image: the dreamer has been put away for doing something bad. If a child came to me with this sort of dream, indicating such deep confusion, I would

immediately sit down and discuss any deep feelings of
insecurity he or she may have. Things need to be made
clearer on all levels for him to feel capable of working out
who he is.

---

Sensitive parents will notice when a child is
struggling with a developmental leap. The best
response to a child's contrariness or perceived
'naughtiness' is to firmly but gently re-establish the
boundaries, bearing in mind that these boundaries
need to be flexible enough to accommodate a grubby-
fingered breach. Sensible parents will foresee possible
problems and do their best to protect the child from
them. For instance, there is no point in leaving a
toddler alone in a room full of priceless china.
Children need to explore and expand their
experience of self, and should be able to do so with
relative abandon.

## Sexual Identity

One of the most important but provocative conflicts
in the child's drive to independence is what Freud
called the *Oedipal conflict*, which crops up time and
again in the dream life of children. ('Oedipal' refers to
the Greek myth of Oedipus, who murdered his father
and married his mother.)

Freud postulated that the little boy incestuously

loves his mother and identifies with his father. The boy notices that his mother does not possess the same genitalia as himself and thinks she has been castrated. The boy fears his father will also castrate him in revenge because of his desires for his mother. In the case of a little girl, Freud maintained that she loves and identifies with the mother, but, noticing that she does not possess the external genitalia of the father, blames the mother for her castration. The girl begins to prefer the father, who possesses the organ she is missing. She then becomes jealous of the mother's relationship with the father.

Around the ages of five to seven, the Oedipal relationship is normally resolved, and the child makes a gender identification with the parent of the same sex.

Some parents find this theory as far-fetched as their children's dreams of monsters and aliens. However, all parents will have at least an inkling that it is essential, from time to time, to suspend disbelief when it comes to the workings of a child's mind. It is critical that parents understand that this psychological drama – described by Freud in terms of a powerful myth – occurs unconsciously. While it does not occur literally in the daily activities of a child's life, it may occur symbolically in his or her relationships with those most essential of beings, the parents.

This theory is much more complex and detailed than the potted version I have set out, and there are many books on the subject you may wish to refer to. There are also other psychological schools of thought on the issue, including modern behavioural psychologists who believe that sex roles are learned by the same processes as other behaviours, that is, by imitating the parents, with its attendant reward and punishment.

Suffice to say that children and parents share a passionate relationship. As they learn physical independence and emerge from the helpless state, children are still subject to momentous psychic ties to their parents. It is impossible to underestimate the power that parents have over the minds and hearts of their children.

This identification with and love of their parents, coupled with immaturity, can make independence a difficult endeavour. The process of separation from parents, and the mythical power struggles that this process entails, may give rise to disturbing dreams. Parents need to be aware of this push-and-pull process, and allow that its effect may be played out in the dream life of their children.

For little girls, positive identification with the mother is essential to establish a robust sense of self-esteem. The early physical relationship with the mother is particularly important as the girl develops a strong sense of what it is to be female. At the same time, she needs to assert her own developing identity. For instance, when young girls play with dolls, much of this play is a form of role-playing of the mother that the girl understands that she will eventually be. In the same way, fathers act as a reference point for boys to model their gender and sexual identity. For example, fathers teach boys about urinating, and about the limits of aggression in play and sport.

As we will discover in Chapter 6, children's dreams are definitely gender specific. What parents need to remember is that it is not so much the politics of the role model that is all-important in childhood (although that may become a bone of contention later, in adolescence), but rather, that the role model – mother or father – exists in some positive form.

## Sibling Rivalry

The presence of siblings is one of the major influences in a child's life. It is through their relationship with brothers and sisters that children learn much about love, consideration and cooperation, and how to resolve emotional conflicts. One of the most problematic of these conflicts is jealousy. According to Winnicott:

> One thing the only child especially lacks is the experience of finding hate turn up; the child's own hate, as the new baby threatens what seems to be a settled and safe relation to the mother and father. It is so usual as to be called normal when a child is upset at the birth of a

new one. The child's first comment is not usually polite: 'It's got a face like a tomato'; in fact, parents should feel relieved when they hear the direct expression of conscious dislike, and even violent hate, at the birth of a new child. This hate will gradually give way to love as the new infant develops into a human being who can be played with, and of whom one can be proud . . . Children who grow up together play games of all kinds, and so have a chance to come to terms with their own aggressiveness, and they have valuable opportunities for discovering on their own that they mind when they really hurt someone they love. (D.W. Winnicott, *The Child, the Family and the Outside World*, page 133.)

---

*I've had three dreams where I kill my baby brother and my older brother. In these dreams I awake crying. Please tell me what they mean. (Scared, 8)*

The middle child often suffers from a feeling of being overlooked. Killing siblings is quite common in children's dreams, but it is very disturbing for the dreamer. The dreamer's parents need to take a little bit more time with this child, and let him or her play out this resentment in more positive and constructive ways. The dreamer may need more encouragement in his or her daily activities.

---

After parents, siblings are the closest relationships that a child is likely to have. The sibling relationship is defined on the one hand by frustration at not receiving the parents' whole attention, and on the other by fraternal love and the sharing of experience that only the sibling bond can give. Once again, a child is forced to monitor extremes of feeling, and the resulting ambivalence is likely to cause tension. Aggression, competitive behaviour and dreams of sibling rivalry are common responses to this conflict.

## How to identify sibling rivalry dreams

In its simplest form, the dreamer expresses hostility by dreaming that the sibling is hurt in some way. In most instances, it is not actually the dreamer who does the deed, but some other agent – a monster, stranger or any other threatening figure. If the dreamer is personally destroying or hurting the sibling, the implications are more serious. If your child is *constantly* dreaming of killing or hurting his or her sibling, the jealousy would appear to have reached dangerous proportions. These are grounds for professional advice. However, if the dream is a one-off, there is no real cause for concern. Usually, this sort of gruesome dream shocks the dreamer more than the parents!

Sometimes, the dreamer is hurt by the sibling or the sibling's agent. This sort of dream is an expression of hostility or fear. The dreamer may be masking his or her sense of rivalry, knowing that it is unacceptable. Or the dreamer has a real awareness of the sibling's capacity to feel jealousy and ability to be hurt.

Sometimes, friends are used as representatives of the resented siblings. Usually, these dreams indicate an intense competitiveness. Patricia Garfield points to the research of Haim Ginott, who found that if sibling rivalry is not worked through in childhood, 'they [the dreamer in question] may go through life treating other people as though they were substitute siblings' (Patricia Garfield, *Your Child's Dreams*, page 162). The implication is that their friendships will be competitive and unsatisfactory and marred by more or less sublimated aggression.

## What to do about sibling rivalry dreams

In families of more than one child, sibling rivalry is as much a rite of passage as Oedipal conflict and separation from parents. Sibling rivalry can be an obsessive issue for children, even in families otherwise unaffected by problems. It is essential for parents to recognise the nature of sibling rivalry, and to take steps to keep the peace, psychologically as well as physically, of all their children. If your child is experiencing sibling rivalry dreams, the time has come to take action in the way you respond to conflicts between your children.

Firstly, accept that the rivalry exists. Remember that children are particularly vulnerable to the demands of their own aggression, and that a mature appraisal of the situation will not be possible until they are into their teens. Parental acceptance of the presence of rivalry is most important. Apart from unpleasant dreams and psychological implications, sibling rivalry can have very serious physical implications. Children who are enraged by jealousy are not moderate about being cruel, particularly if the focus of their assault is a sibling who is perceived – for whatever reason – to be favoured by parents.

Secondly, take the dreams seriously and take action to rebalance the situation. It is up to parents to moderate the behaviours between the children until they are able to moderate their own behaviour.

Under no circumstances should one child be favoured over another. If you, as a parent, are aware that you sometimes play favourites, take constructive steps to resolve the problem. Do not compare the children's abilities and achievements. Comparisons are more than odious, they are damaging. Foster each child's sense of confidence by nurturing and praising them for their specific and unique talents. Give each child special attention.

If a child is showing signs of depression – for instance, through falling school grades, anxiety, loss of appetite, poor sleep and nightmares – or complains of feeling overwhelmed or attacked by siblings, then you must investigate. It is important that all the children know that bullying is unacceptable, at any time, in any way.

## Aggression

Unrestrained outbursts of anger and aggression are entirely normal, if troublesome, aspects of the developing child. Anger and aggression are linked to a sense of frustration on the one hand, and a sense of power on the other.

As a drive, aggression is one of the most basic and useful for children. Feelings of aggression encourage the child to seek for food, to suck hard, to persist. Later, it urges the child to push at the boundaries of what he or she knows: to sit, to walk, to express him or herself, to achieve goals. Aggression, in this positive, energetic form, is present in every child and should be channelled and directed. According to Winnicott, it is these early infantile hittings that:

> lead to a discovery of the world that is not the infant's self, and to the beginnings of a relationship to external objects. What will quite soon be aggressive behaviour is therefore at the start a simple impulse that leads to a movement and to the beginnings of exploration. Aggression is always linked in this way with the establishment of a clear distinction between what is the self and what is not the self. (D.W. Winnicott, *The Child, the Family and the Outside World*, page 234.)

Destructive impulses can be useful. The tendency to destroy is linked to the ability to create: these are two sides of the same coin. The timid, over-controlled child who may feel he or she is not allowed to experiment does not properly learn the boundaries of hostility or the joys of simple aggressive experimentation, such as the feeling that comes when destroying a beloved toy and trying to put it back together again, or scribbling over a favourite book. Aggression remains a frightening concept – ever-present, but unexplored. This child may have unpleasantly violent dreams (here I should say that *all* children have violent dreams, but some are more bothered by them than others) to expel some of this pent-up energy, or an un-characteristic, explosive temper tantrum that is so frightening the child may not remember a thing about the episode.

---

*My dream was that my mother and I were in a car, but paddling, trying to get away from my father. The next thing, my mother was in the kitchen drying the knives and forks. My father was in the hallway having a go at me when my mother just turned around with a knife in her hand and said, 'Leave her alone'. The next thing I knew, my father was getting the scissors out of the drawer and began stabbing my mother in the back. I grabbed another knife and started stabbing my father. While I was stabbing him I was laughing and asking Mum if she was all right. I woke up after my father had fallen to the ground. I was so happy to see that my mother was fine because my dream seemed so real. My father was drunk in the dream. (Daughter, 12)*

I wonder if violence is a part of family life in this home. There seems to be a link with alcohol. The aggression being shown in the dream probably indicates a lot of sublimated aggression. The dreamer is feeling worried for her mother, and is very protective of her. Perhaps the father is domineering; perhaps there is a complicity between mother and daughter. In any case, the images are very strong and indicate that a serious discussion about family relationships is due. More drastic action may be necessary.

---

So, aggressive expression is important, just as developing self-control is important. A child who does not learn to withhold hostility and regulate his or her own aggression wins only short-term concessions. For instance, the child throws a tantrum and the mother gives in and buys him or her an ice-cream. Or the child is allowed to bully and stand-over the timid children in the playground. Such a child may learn, erroneously, that aggression is about self-aggrandisement, and does not learn to consider others.

Every parent knows that temper tantrums and outbursts of destructive energy are prevalent at various stages of a child's development. It is sometimes hard to both allow and contain the anger and aggression of a child. It is even harder for children to learn to contain themselves. A constructive parental response is to encourage creative alternatives such as drawing, playing and discussion. See Chapter 5 for strategies on how to encourage creative activity in dreams.

Many, many children write to me about their violent and aggressive dreams. In fact, most children's dreams have a high percentage of violent, aggressive and sometimes gruesome activity. As Winnicott says:

> In another more mature alternative to aggressive behaviour the child dreams. In dreaming, destruction and killing are experienced in fantasy, and this dreaming is associated with any degree of excitement in the body, and is a real experience and not just an intellectual exercise. The child who can manage dreams is becoming ready for all kinds of playing, either alone or with other children. If the dream contains too much destruction or involves too severe a threat to sacred objects, or if chaos supervenes, then the child wakes screaming. Here the mother [or father] plays [a] part by being available and by helping the child to wake from the nightmare so that external reality may play its reassuring part once more. This process of waking may take the child the best part of half an hour. The nightmare itself may be a strangely satisfactory experience for the child. (D.W. Winnicott, *The Child, the Family and the Outside World*, page 235.)

Winnicott prefigures another outlet for aggressive impulse – play. Both dreaming and playing suggest that a child is able to *visualise* at some level so that the conflicts of love and hate that he or she is feeling for the mother or the new baby, for example, are released.

Dreams and play allow children to express dangerous, contradictory emotions in symbolic form. Children may not even be aware that they are symbolising. All they know is that they dream and play, and that the processes of dreaming and playing offer them some release. The acts allow them to explore the relationship between destroying something and creating something. That is, unless some other unhealthy dynamic is operating, when the dreams or playing become disturbed and the child achieves no release, just more anxiety. If this is the case, then parents are advised to seek professional counsel.

According to Winnicott:

> Plenty of time is needed for a baby and child to master aggressive ideas and excitements and to be able to control them without losing the ability to be aggressive at appropriate moments, whether in hating or in loving.
>
> Oscar Wilde said 'Each man kills the thing he loves'. It is brought to our notice every day that along with loving we must expect hurting. In child care we see that children tend to love the thing they hurt. Hurting is very much a part of child life, and the question is: how will your child find a way of harnessing those aggressive forces to the task of living, loving, playing and (eventually) working? (D.W. Winnicott, *The Child, the Family and the Outside World*, page 237.)

## SUMMARY

☼ Dreams are indicators of the emotional aspects of a child's development.

☼ Ideally, children grow to have a harmonious concept of Self. This concept has been described by Freud as having three parts: the id, or the inner, subjective Self, which dominates in childhood; the ego, or the director of the Self, which balances all the demands of a personality; and the superego, or the system of values or morals of the Self.

☼ A child has key phases of emotional growth which are characterised by learning trust, control, inventiveness and competence.

☼ Language is one of the most important tools a child can learn. It is connected to the development of memory, perception, judgement and the ability to think. It allows children to articulate their internal life and dreams.

☼ Children learn objectivity gradually. At first, they do not understand the separation of inner and outer states, or dreaming and waking.

☼ Anxiety is common in childhood and accompanies all aspects of growth. If allowed to dominate, it can be destructive to a child's development. Anxiety is one of the most common dream feelings for a child.

☼ The struggle to separate from parents is one in which all children engage and one which is fraught with difficulty. The Oedipal conflict is central to a child's growing independence and often figures in dreams.

☼ Some psychologists think that sexual identity is based on imitation of parents. Role-modelling happens through the child's identification with the parent of the same sex.

☼ Sibling rivalry is another unpleasant but common factor of childhood and is often played out in dreams. There are various actions parents can take to cope with and minimise the effects of sibling rivalry within a family.

☼ Aggression is a basic drive, and is very common in the dream-life of children. A child needs to learn gradually to modulate aggression with self-control.

# 3

## NIGHTMARES, NIGHT TERRORS, BAD DREAMS AND HOW TO DEAL WITH THEM

### What is a Nightmare?

Nightmares are bad dreams, but worse. They are usually bad enough to cause a child to wake in fright. They are usually more graphic and elaborate, involving greater anxiety and physical activity. The dreamer's survival is often threatened. Nightmares are, to a large extent, the 'normal' accompaniments of certain developmental trends in childhood, and express anxieties caused by the demands of growing up. A nightmare is usually very graphic, and children will often remember key details that they may find extremely disturbing.

Say your son wakes from a nightmare (as distinct from a night terror, see pages 55–7). He will be upset and frightened, and perhaps crying. He will have the images still in his head, and he will usually be coherent enough to sort them out and tell you at the time. (The child's ability to relate the dream will improve as his linguistic abilities improve.) On the other hand, he may find it difficult to discuss the *feelings* behind the dream there and then. Leave it till the morning to sort through the special reasons for the nightmare's occurrence and the feelings behind it.

With nightmares, the child has usually been asleep for around half the night. Most nightmares are reported in children between seven and ten years old, but I feel that this is because a child is more able, by this age, to describe the details to the parents. In fact, it appears that nightmares can occur from the age of nine months old, sometimes as young as six months.

## Why do nightmares occur?

Nightmares are usually a response to stress in the child's life. This can be stress involved with daily life and the demands it places on the child, or it can be unusual stresses, including changes in family life such as the parents' separation or divorce or death in the family; an addition to the family (a new baby or a step-sibling or step-parent); a change of school or abode; unusual social friction with a new classmate or a new configuration of friends.

Nightmares are compensatory (see Chapter 1). They attempt to expel some of the energy of the stress, which is pent-up in the unconscious. As always, the unconscious is a faithful monitor of what is really happening in the psyche.

Therefore nightmares can be salutary, indicating

an area for concern, and inviting parents to examine an issue more closely with their child. However, if the nightmare is extremely frightening, the challenge for a parent is to coax the child to 'revisit' the episode – it may be so traumatic that the child simply wants to avoid discussion. Avoidance is not good policy, however. A bad dream or nightmare will often recur until the reasons for it are teased out and dealt with.

Another reason for nightmares may be physical. Certain physical states seem to increase the likelihood of nightmares, including:

- drug withdrawal (if the child has been medicated for some time, then he or she may experience nightmares after medication is stopped)
- high fever
- fatigue
- indigestion
- allergies
- hypersensitivity (some children are more sensitive to their environment than others; a very sensitive individual will react to changes or demands by having nightmares, where a more sanguine little personality will not)
- family association (nightmares seem to run in families, so if you are prone to nightmares it is likely that your child will be also).

## What parents should do about nightmares

Initially, when (say) your daughter wakes from a nightmare, she may be unclear about where she is. She may be terrified that the monster or other offending personage is in the room (see Chapter 2). Reassure and comfort your child straightaway to dispel the fears. Younger children may need to be shown that neither the curtains nor the bed are hiding the culprit. Turn on the light and sit the child up. Walk her around the room to inspect it. Do all that is required to situate her in the here and now, which is probably around 3 a.m. in her own bedroom!

Then, gently elicit as many details of the dream as possible, without reawakening the anxiety. Note them down for discussion later.

When you put your child back to bed and settle her once again, suggest a positive outcome should the monster return. This alternative outcome must not be too complex. For example, you could suggest that your child tell the monster loudly not to bother her any more, and tell it to run away. Or she could confront the monster and ask him why he is chasing her. Or you could suggest that the monster might be friendly, and perhaps the child could make a new friend. ·

Ask your child to rehearse briefly whatever solution seems best. Then, encourage your child to go back to sleep.

Remember that children are very suggestible, particularly when suggestions come from parents. Use this characteristic to foster confidence and positivity in their dream lives.

## Ongoing nightmare therapy

1 **Encourage confrontation.** Work with your child on positive ways to conquer the monster. After your initial response at the time of the nightmare, take the time to discuss the nightmare further with your child the next day. Ask how he or she felt, and if he or she could think of things to say to the monster. Can your child think of a way in which the monster may be defeated or be made less frightening? By discussing alternative outcomes with your child, you will discover a great deal more detail about the nightmare, and encourage the imagination of positive resources.

2 **Call for help.** Your child may feel more comfortable with the idea of calling for help in a nightmare, so suggest people or animals he or she can look to for aid. Parents, a strong, older sibling, a favourite big dog or even a character from a fairy story or favourite film can be candidates. Discuss how the hero or heroine can act to overcome fear. Suggest to your child that he or she can be the hero or heroine in the dream.

3 **Stories before bedtime.** Choose stories where the protagonist is successful after adversity. (See Chapter 6 for the positive power of fairytales.) Be mindful of what television programmes your child is exposed to before bedtime. For further information on the effect of the media on children and their dreams, see Chapter 6.

4 **Relive the dream in waking imagination.** This is one of the most effective ways of changing disturbing dream patterns. Firstly, sit down with your child and remember together all the details of the nightmare. Ask your child to draw the dream, including as many details as possible.

Discuss positive ways in which the dream could be resolved, and let your child choose the best one for him or her. Ask your child to draw the dream with the new ending so that he or she is compelled to confront and overcome the anxiety about the nightmare. The child will realise that he or she is able to imagine different approaches to the problem, and therefore use his or her own resources to change the outcome of the dream. Suggest that your child uses the positive alternative dream should the nightmare return.

This same pattern can be repeated in other creative forms: in role-playing for example, or dance, or play with dolls and toys. All of these methods allow your child to work out the elements of the dream that are disturbing, and to change them constructively.

5 **Learn about the fearful object or event.** Research has shown that children who explore the nature of their fears are able to overcome their nightmares. So, if the nightmare involves a large, frightening lion, the parent should encourage the child to find out as much as possible about lions – where they are found, their habits and actions. If the nightmare involves fire or men with weapons, parents can assist the child by visiting a fire or police station. Children's natural curiosity will lead them into a more positive relationship with the feared object or event if they are encouraged to explore it in waking life.

6 **Sleep rituals.** Many nightmares are provoked by anxiety about change. It is very important that bedtime involves some pleasant rituals. In this way, even if change is invading other areas of their life, they are able to focus on a time in the day when everything is predictable and exactly as it should be. Rituals of going to bed also help prevent sleep problems and bolster confidence against fear of the dark.

Try to make sure that children are put to bed at roughly the same time every night, apart from 'treat' nights when an eagerly anticipated event will override normal bedtime hours. There should be a ritual to the sequence of events; for example, dinner, bath, teeth brushed, story reading (choose positive outcome stories), saying goodnight to family and toys, and lights out. Some parents encourage children to say prayers before sleep.

If your child is afraid of the dark, you may consider leaving a weak night light on in the room, or outside the room with the door ajar.

A child's bed and bedroom should be predictable. If this is not always possible, choose a favourite sleep toy or special blanket to accompany the child to bed. This way, should the child awake disoriented, he or she will find a familiar cuddly object with which he or she associates sleep, warmth and safety. See Chapter 5 for further discussion of bedtime rituals.

7 **Always attend to a child who has suffered a nightmare.** Never leave a child to cry alone in the middle of the night. Children, especially very young children, will sometimes wake in the night and agitate a little for attention. This is a totally different issue. Small children need to learn to go back to sleep after waking normally so that they establish good sleep patterns.

However, when your child has had a nightmare (and you will know this even without being told by the insistence of the crying and obvious distress of the child) it is essential that parental support be provided. A solid trust in their parents' protection is important to bolster children's confidence.

Children have to learn what is real and what is

imagined, and even for adults who know the difference, a nightmare can be very frightening.

It is important not to negate, dismiss or belittle a child's nightmare. It is much more productive to go through the event than to brush it off as simply a dream. The nightmare may then turn into a recurring problem that is much more difficult to unseat.

8 **Discuss dreams with your children.** Dream discussion can foster a very precious dialogue with your children, and establishes a close link with their fears and insecurities. It also gives you a window to their hopes and desires. It is important to discuss all dreams with your children, or all the dreams that they bring you. Good dreams can be marvellous ways of raising confidence and hope. You can use the methods described above to encourage creativity from good dreams as well as bad.

## Night Terrors

Night terrors are different to nightmares in a number of ways. The strongest characteristic of a night terror is that a child wakes in a state of extreme terror. Usually the child:

- wakes suddenly, with a loud scream
- may sit up, get out of bed, or exhibit agitated physical response

- perspires heavily and breathes rapidly
- has a very rapid heartbeat
- may appear to be hallucinating, with dilated pupils, and eyes open but unseeing
- is inconsolable for several minutes, even up to half an hour
- cannot recall any imagery of the terror, or rarely a single, overwhelming vision
- cannot recall terror at all in the morning.

Night terrors generally happen early in the night. The child has usually only been asleep for about an hour or two at the onset of the terror. These attacks happen most often in the two to five-year-old age group. They are rare, occurring in only 1 to 5 per cent of children.

## What causes night terrors?

Night terrors are episodes that happen in very deep sleep, not REM sleep, as most dreams do. There has been some suggestion that attacks could be brought on by fever, head injury or emotional stress, or by an immature nervous system, but there are no clear links. They are slightly more common in male children and very occasionally indicate the presence of mild epilepsy. Children generally outgrow night terrors. If the attacks become frequent, then medical advice is essential.

## What parents should do about night terrors

Although night terrors can be extremely alarming for parents, it is important to remember that they have no ill-effects, and it is likely your child will not recall any of the episode in the morning.

Move slowly and gently, and speak to your child in a soothing, low voice. Your child may be thrashing about or moving restlessly. Do not forcibly restrain the child (who may still be immersed in the terror), but stroke and contain him or her within a room if possible.

Do not attempt to 'rouse' the child by slapping or shouting – he or she is in an hallucinatory state. Gentle, firm tones are more likely to calm.

Let the child return to sleep as soon as possible without too much inquiry.

## Ongoing night terror therapy

Unfortunately, there is very little parents can do. While children will most likely outgrow these episodes, perhaps you may want to discreetly examine the security surrounding your child. However, if night terrors are frequent, then medical advice must be sought.

In the rare case of night terror in adults, victims are advised to increase their sense of security in both physical and psychological terms.

## Bad Dreams

Bad dreams happen to everyone regardless of age. For children who suffer frequently from bad dreams, night-time may be accompanied with a growing sense of dread. While bad dreams may not cause as much overt disruption as nightmares, their effect can be insidious. A child may feel so weighed down by borderline anxiety that he or she becomes depressed.

If your child shows signs of anxiety or continued sleeplessness at night, or any symptoms of depression including withdrawal, loss of spontaneity or poor grades at school, then parents should inquire gently as to the content of his or her dreams. Ongoing therapy for bad dreams is the same as for nightmares.

## SUMMARY

☀ Nightmares are dreams bad enough for a child to wake in fright. They express anxieties that are common in growing children. Certain key details will be remembered that will be very disturbing for the child. Often, the child's survival will be threatened in the dream.

☀ Nightmares occur from a very early age. They usually take place about halfway through a child's normal night sleep. A child will recall the nightmare in the morning and this is the best time to discuss the dream in detail.

☀ Nightmares are reactions to stress. They may also have physical causes.

☀ Parental response to a child's nightmare should be prompt and reassuring, and should include a suggested positive action that the child can take should the dream recur. There are various steps parents can take on an ongoing basis to deal with nightmares which include discussion of alternative endings to the nightmare, reading positive stories before bedtime, drawing the dream, learning about the fearful object or event, developing bedtime rituals and general dream discussion.

☀ Night terrors are different from nightmares and generally happen early in the night, are accompanied by a state of extreme physical agitation, and are generally never remembered by the child in the morning. Luckily, night terrors are rare, and occur mostly in the two to five-year-old age group.

☀ Response to night terrors should be soothing and calm. Encourage your child to return to sleep as soon as possible.

☀ Bad dreams are a matter of degree. If your child is suffering from bad dreams, then use the same therapy as for nightmares.

# 4

## DREAMS AND WHAT THEY MEAN

More than adults, children dream thematically. This may be connected to the strongly archetypal nature of children's dreams. Within these themes, each child will bring his or her own particular images and messages.

It is essential to remember that there are no strict formulas for dream analysis. Each dream is unique to the dreamer, which means that the dreamer is best placed to work out the dream. The following discussion will serve as a guide, and aims to deepen your understanding of how dreams work. Use this as a starting point for discussions with your child.

There are two major problems with children's dreams: first, the dreamer may not be objective or mature enough to unravel the meanings of his or her dream. Or, the dreamer may not be able to explain clearly what happened in the dream because of linguistic immaturity. On the other hand, the thematic nature of children's dreams lends itself more easily to analysis from a sympathetic third party – and who better than a child dreamer's parents?

Children seem to remember far more bad dreams

than good. This is probably because bad dreams are disturbing, and leave them with a sense of troubled anxiety all day. Also, bad dreams are likely to be more frequent because the child is subject to pressures while growing up, which cause anxiety that in turn needs to be discharged. Bad dreams are like letting off steam as the unconscious attempts to solve problems of the psyche. Children are generally not in control of their emotions as adults are, or are not practised at diverting or compartmentalising them, so emotions tend to seem more frightening and unwieldy. Children's dreams often reflect this discomfort.

## Animals

Unlike adult dreams, children's dreams are teeming with animals. For children between three and five, animals are the major actors in dreams, and the action is likely to be violent. Hardly any people appear in dreams of children in this age group. As children grow, animals become less frequent. It has been found that children over the age of seven who dream frequently of animals are often less socially adept than average.

Children's animal dreams are likely to feature beasts of which the dreamer is frightened. So, for young children, animal dreams are often nightmarish or very bad. David Foulkes, in his landmark study on children's dreams, concluded that as children mature, their dream animals become easier to manage. This is a vital clue to the meaning of animals in dreams: they represent the nature of the child's primitive instincts and emotions. They are characters of the childish Freudian id.

---

*I am twelve and ever since I went on a wild pig-shooting spree I have been having bad dreams about pigs and dingoes coming to get me. They never attack me but they chase me and they seem to be everywhere I turn. Please tell me what my dreams mean. (ABC, 12)*

Being chased in dreams is one of the most common dream experiences. The dreamer feels pursued by the animals. Generally, this image suggests to me peer group pressure and a crisis of identity. The dramatic way in which the dreamer came across these animals (that is, on a shooting spree) has helped her subconscious hold onto the pictures for dream reference. I would like to know more about how the dreamer felt about the shooting spree. I imagine it was very gruesome. Perhaps the dreamer feels guilty. Where are the dingoes from? I would like to know more about the dreamer's feelings about dingoes. There is some fear in the dreamer's life that she needs to turn and face.

*I have quite a few dreams, all different, but the common factor of these dreams is dolphins. They are always in danger and I help to rescue them. I feel upset for them and helpless in the dream but upon waking I have a wonderful feeling because of the mystical aura*

*surrounding these lovely creatures. In the dream, they*
*seem to understand me too. (Jane, 12)*

The tone and feeling of this dream on waking really stand
out. All dreams, whether funny, sad or frightening, leave us
with a feeling when we wake. This appears to be a very
positive dream, which the dreamer has connected with
feelings of the spirit. The dolphins are in danger, but they
are rescued. There seems to be a communication between
the dreamer and the dolphins. What is it that the dolphins
represent for the dreamer? What attributes do they have?
Answering these questions will perhaps establish why the
dolphins are in danger and need to be rescued.

*I am an eleven-year-old girl and I had a dream about a*
*friend of mine who, the day before, I had a*
*disagreement with. In the dream I was at the school*
*oval with a girl in my class and my friend. I got up and*
*walked over to a small pool in which I heard a snake*
*talking. It was saying it would bite the girl in my class*
*who was about to have a drink from the pool. He bit*
*her, but nothing happened. My friend got up from her*
*drink and I saw two distinct marks on either side of her*
*nose. I was extremely frightened for her life, because I*
*knew the snake was poisonous so I screamed to*
*someone to call the ambulance while I helped her up*
*the hill to the car park. A man came from the*
*ambulance and took her away. I was terrified that she*
*would die. (Chloe, 11)*

It seems the dreamer may be very worried about the fight she has had with her friend. I wonder if the fight was about jealousy. I suspect the dreamer feels guilty, and thinks she may have mortally wounded her friend. The snake here is, I think, projected bad feeling. The friend does not know that the snake lurks beneath the water where she is taking a drink. It would be interesting to know what associations the dreamer has with the snake in her dream, and how she feels about the friendship which has suffered a rupture.

---

Patricia Garfield's view is that children see animals as having a freedom that they may not have. 'Animals need not control their hunger or their bowels or their sexual feelings, as parents insist children do. Sometimes animals can successfully deny parental authority in ways rarely available to children. Vicariously, the child triumphs' (Patricia Garfield, *Your Child's Dreams*, page 44).

Animals carry enormous archetypal significance in dreams. Primitive tribes worshipped animal totems and signified spiritual connection by the presence of animal messengers in dreams. Bruno Bettelheim sums up the two sorts of archetypal energy attached to animals found in fairytales:

Both dangerous and helpful animals stand for our animal nature, our instinctual drives. The dangerous ones symbolise the untamed id, not yet subjected to ego and superego control, in all its dangerous energy. The

> helpful animals represent our natural energy – again the id – but now made to serve the best interests of the total personality. There are also some animals, usually white birds such as doves, which symbolise the superego. (Bruno Bettelheim, *The Uses of Enchantment*, page 76.)

Animals in fairytales have a similar symbolic function to animals in children's dreams.

Dreams featuring animal friends and guides are usually pleasant for children. Often, the animal will lead them out of a difficult situation, or show them where to find something they have been seeking. Sometimes, the child will just spend time playing with and talking to the animal. These dreams may represent your child coming to terms with his or her instincts, and allowing them to be used creatively as well as destructively.

## What specific animals may represent

The following list is really only for your information. Beware of making assumptions about the symbolic meaning of the animals appearing in your children's dreams. As far as possible, allow the child to explain to you his or her feelings about the animal or animals that feature. Avoid suggesting meanings – children are very suggestible. If your child cannot explain or describe in words either because he or she is too young or blocked in some way, try drawing or role-playing the scenario instead. Ask your child:

- what he or she feels about the animal
- to describe the animal
- to talk about the attributes – good and bad – of the animal.

Remember that cultural attitudes may influence feelings your child has about the animal in question.

Here is a list of some of the animals that frequently feature in children's dreams and what they may mean.

**Birds**  Flight into another dimension; freedom; escape. Maybe spiritual transcendence. In children, may indicate the development of the superego.

**Cat**  Can mean a number of things, depending on the child's relationship to them. Traditionally associated with the moon, female wisdom and intuition. Can be the cuddly, fluffy family pet, but a cat usually carries mystical connotations.

**Dog**  Friendly, faithful, instinctive; intermediary between humans and their instinct. Human beings' best friend. A wild dog is quite different, however, displaying ferocity that a child is likely to find terrifying.

**Fish**  Inevitably connected with water; symbolising the emotions, the life force, the unconscious. An ancient fertility symbol, often representing sperm. Symbolically: abundance. The fisherman in traditional folklore is often wise.

**Horse**  For children, the horse may represent wildness tamed. Horses are extremely powerful, and may cause fear, but they can be ridden and managed. Symbolically, they represent the power of the instincts to operate in the conscious world. Traditionally associated with magic, the wind, the underworld, and water.

**Lions and tigers**  Rulers of the jungle; animal passions that can devour the dreamer. Most lion and tiger dreams are about the power of these animals to eat the child. However, most children are also impressed by the beauty of lions and tigers, and their symbolic position at the top of the jungle hierarchy.

**Snake**  An archetypal symbol with a myriad connotations, the snake can mean different things to different children at different times. It is very important that children who dream of snakes explain their own special feelings about them because symbolically, snakes are very complex creatures. Has obvious sexual or gender connotations for young boys, who may be both fearful of, and fascinated by, snakes. In many mythologies, the snake represents very basic primal energy – the kundalini energy of the belly in eastern mysticism that lies at the base of the spine and energises the chakras, for example. Also associated with feminine as well as masculine forces. Can be evil, but has always been associated with healing and regeneration (probably through the shedding of skin). This very complex symbol can also indicate negative emotions that feed on themselves.

**Spiders** Another creature that has both good and bad properties symbolically. Children may marvel at the beauty of a spider's web, but squirm at the sight of a spider devouring its prey. Spiders are yucky, but compelling.

## Strangers

Many children's dreams are dominated by a threatening figure who endangers the dreamer in some way. I shall call this figure the Stranger. Usually, the Stranger is male, although some threatening female figures have been reported also. The female figures usually take the form of witches. The Stranger is powerful and potentially deadly. Sometimes the Stranger takes action in the dream, attempting to harm the dreamer in some way. Sometimes the Stranger is just a presence who fills the child with dread. What does this figure represent?

---

*I have a recurring nightmare of my mum standing in front of me with her eyes wide open and bloodshot. She had her finger pointing right in my face. It terrifies me so much that I even have the nightmare when wide awake during the day. (AQ, 8)*

The dreamer may have been unfairly disciplined by his mother or had some disagreement that has caused both anger and fear. Mother, with whom the dreamer is very angry, must be cast as a horror otherwise the dreamer may be overwhelmed by his emotions. As it is, this is a very potent dream and he is very afraid. He needs to speak to his mother about the dream. Because he may be too scared to do so, I suggest she needs to become more sensitive to the dreamer's needs. A child having recurring dreams of this sort will show other signs of distress.

---

In many ways, the Stranger is an archetypal symbol. Just as animals may represent the untrammelled instincts, the Stranger is the child's fear of larger, stronger adults who may not always have the child's best interests at heart. The Stranger is the Baddie. He may wear any number of costumes, but he is always frightening. He will often be dressed in black, or take the form of an evil-doer from a movie or book who has made a particular impression on the child, for instance, Dracula.

If your child dreams of the Stranger, it probably means that there is some conflict occurring in his or her daily life with an authority figure. The classic ambivalence of the child between the need to rebel and the need to conform means that authority figures can be greatly feared as well as loved. The setting of the dream – home, school, sports field – will give you a strong clue as to where the conflict lies.

Very often, the conflict lies at home and it is a big

shock for some parents to discover that the Stranger is often a disguise for the parents themselves.

It is dangerous for children to defy their mother or father. They realise that they may lose love or be cast out. The feelings of anger or rebellion may manifest in dreams, especially if they are not able or allowed or it is inappropriate for them to discharge their emotions in everyday life. It is safer if parents are cast into a disguise in frightening dreams rather than making guest appearances as themselves. Thus the mother, who may have been angry with the child that day, becomes the Witch. Father, who thundered at the child over bad school results, may appear as the Incredible Hulk, crushing everything before him.

---

*I am eleven years old and had a dream that a man was living with us. I thought he was a spy. One night my brother ran up the stairs yelling, 'He's a Spanish man!' Then we ran out the door. What does this mean? (Eric, 11)*

This dream represents a fear of the foreigner, probably the foreigner within, as he is living with the family. This stranger may be a projection of the dreamer, or somehow a projection of a part of the brother. I would like to know more about the associations that the dreamer makes with spies and Spanish men in particular. Has he been watching a movie? Is something happening within the family which is making him suspicious about an intruder? What is going on in the immediate environment of the dreamer? Was he scared in the dream or not?

*I am nine years old and my mother said I could write to you because I have been having a very bad dream all the time. I am in a forest with lots of trees with my cousin and my sister. A bald man with an axe is trying to chase us and then kill us. We all split up and then my dream ends. (Lisa, 9)*

This dream seems to be related to some kind of hidden fear the dreamer is experiencing. Although her cousin and her sister are with her in the beginning of the dream, by the end of the dream they have split up and she is alone. What is her relationship to these relatives in waking life? The forest is a potent symbol here: there are lots of trees (making visibility difficult, I would imagine) and I would like this girl to draw the forest, and where the bald man is in it. Tales of axe murderers abound: has she heard something about such a murder that has connected with her imaginative unconscious? I suspect that the family of the dreamer is experiencing unresolved conflicts. As the mother gave permission for the dreamer to write, I would guess that she appreciates that her child is on to something very important. Perhaps the family needs to have an open and frank discussion about conflicts between its members so any undercurrents can be resolved.

The Oedipal struggles of childhood may result in bad dreams of Strangers and Witches. If your child is in the process of separating from the mother, or working out issues with the powerful authority figure of the father, the confusion may throw out images of threatening figures. The establishment of identity boundaries for a child is frightening and often muddled. It is not something that happens overnight, and often children will become more clingy and strident when they realise that life requires them to become more independent. Even little babies feel this pressure and counterpressure of the drive for identity. The conflict of dependence versus independence is the titanic struggle of childhood, and goes on for years.

Parents, friends, siblings, teachers or others in the child's environment who make an appearance as themselves can cause great anxiety to the child. If this situation arises, it is very important to get to the heart of the problem that is haunting your child, even if it is you who is the terrifying figure. Realise that children will naturally be more reluctant to discuss dreams of this sort with you if you are the feature Baddie, so go in gently. It might be more helpful if the child can confide in another close family member.

When examining Stranger dreams, follow the same process as for animal dreams. Ask your child to describe his or her feelings and the figure in the dream, and ask him or her to explain the attributes of the figure. Once you have a strong idea of how the child has seen the dream, get him or her to draw it out or role-play the scenario. Suggest positive alternatives if the dream ended badly.

## A Word on Sexual Abuse

The Stranger appears with significant force in the dreams of children who have been physically abused. This is not to say that parents should be looking for this interpretation of Stranger dreams. Child abuse is a complex, disturbing area, and diagnosis should be left to the experts. If you suspect that your child is being or has been abused, bad dreams may be the first indication. An abused child is often sworn to secrecy by the abuser, and dreams become the only available outlet for the discharge of this poisonous, negative energy. Also, a child will often 'block' abuse trauma, and dreams, in their compensatory function, will attempt to resolve the pain.

---

*I am eighteen years old and I want to tell you that I was sexually molested as a child. I always used to have nightmares about snakes and being chased by them. I heard that dreaming about snakes usually relates to something sexual. When I left home last year to get married I had one final dream that the snakes were being killed by a man. I was wondering if this was my*

*subconscious self telling me that now that I was leaving
the abuse had finally stopped. (Kay, 18)*

Snakes in dreams are strong symbols. They can both kill
and cure, and they represent energy, health, jealousy, evil
and so on. The snake is also a very strong symbol of the
phallus – a sexual symbol. I think that the dreamer has
successfully interpreted the dream and its message.

*Recently I was dreaming I was having a shower with
two other friends. My dad entered and tried to sexually
abuse me but I chased him out and beat him. I was
crying and asking him why he did this and he said for
one of my uncles and that this uncle had pressured him
into doing it. (J, 15)*

I would like to know much more about the family life of this
girl. Perhaps there has actually been abuse, and the girl is
unconsciously trying to find an excuse for her father, hence
the involvement of the uncle. What is her relationship like
with her father? Perhaps the dreamer is suffering unwelcome
attention from the uncle. In any case, with this sort of
dream, I would advise counselling. The images are very
direct, unmasked and disturbing.

---

Sufferers of post-traumatic stress disorder report
that they relive events through dreams, until therapy
and time soften the images. War veterans, people

who have undergone stress through serious accident, and victims of violent crime (and, of course, sexual abuse is a crime of violation) commonly have such dreams.

Children who have been abused report dreams of the actual event or events, but they also report dreams of being suffocated, overwhelmed or trapped in some way. This is the disguise that the dream uses to protect the child from the full, horrifying implication of what has occurred. Guilt, shame and fear are the constant emotional accompaniments to such dreams.

---

*As a child I had a recurring dream about three friends and their families and we would go to a park, where in real life we did go and play hide-and-seek. I would always hide behind a grey shed in my dream and I can't remember what happened next, but I would see an image of meat cut up on a chopping board and I would know it was me. In real life we were stopped from going to this park as strange men used to linger there. I was abused as a kid. Has this dream got anything to do with it? (Dee, 14)*

I would say so, although you don't say whether you were abused by one of the strange men in the park, or someone else. However, certainly, the park became a symbol for you. The chopping board and meat represent the dreamer being cut up and served up to eat in a particularly gruesome way:

probably referring to the feelings of being abused, and having to repress and deny her own self under duress. This dreamer is still carrying the experiences of her childhood and recognising the dream's message is part of the repair for this teenager. She mentions a grey shed: often the colour grey signals a sense of depression.

---

A rape dream does not necessarily mean that the child has been raped, however. In typical dream-like fashion, images of rape can stand for something else. If your child tells you about a rape dream, proceed with great care. The first step is to discuss where this image might have arisen. Has he or she been watching gruesome television shows? Is the dream a result of particularly vivid playground talk? Does he or she have a general curiosity about an emerging sexuality? Once again, the feelings that your child has about the dream and the general state of his or her psyche should be your guide.

Be very careful about drawing any conclusions, however. Dreams can be quite shocking, and often sexuality is used as a metaphor. The Oedipal struggle often gives rise to bizarre and disturbing images. Also remember that for children, there is a fine line between fact and fantasy. If their emerging sexuality is exposed to images of incest and rape, these images may be played with in an experimental fashion. Dreams are primarily symbolic. They must always be seen in the context of the child's general behaviour before any firm conclusions can be drawn.

But if you have strong suspicions that your child is being abused, seek professional help *immediately*.

## Monsters

Monsters are allied to Strangers in dreams, and have archetypal significance, often representing a fear of large outside forces that can be harmful to a child but over which the child has little control. There is another facet to Monster dreams: the frightening figure can often symbolise the child's fear of the destructive forces within him or herself.

Characteristically, a Monster will grab, clutch or eat the dreamer. The Monster may be a unique fabrication of the child's mind – often a polyglot of unpleasant parts – or it can be borrowed from book or film. Frequently, the Monster will live somewhere familiar but frightening, such as a dark enclosed space from which it emerges in the dream. Closets, cupboards, cellars and under the bed are all common Monster hideouts. To some extent, Monsters are manifestations of a more abstract fear common to all children – fear of the dark.

When dealing with Monster dreams, it is very helpful to urge children to draw. Quite often, children will enjoy outing their fear in this way. Once again, a parent should discuss ways of dealing with this

Monster – its attributes and weaknesses, and positive approaches children can take in the dream should it return. If the Monster's home is in the closet, cellar or under the bed, I have found it helpful to inspect the area with the child before bedtime. Another successful ploy is to encourage game playing in and out of the frightening place during the day. Frights can be generated merely by a child's lurid imagination, and if a parent is able to exhaust the possibilities of a potential threat, then all the better.

## Lost or Abandoned

When children dream of being lost or abandoned in any way, it indicates that they are feeling alone and without resources. It is important for parents to note that children experience being lost as being abandoned. To children, these two events are indistinguishable, and are one and the same emotion. Such a dream is very disturbing for children, and heightens the childish fear of helplessness. Children who dream consistently along these lines may feel deserted by their parents. It is quite common for this sort of dream to occur at times of separation and divorce, or at the death of a parent. Children often fear, at the time of separation and divorce, that they have to take sides, or that somehow the failure of the marriage is their fault. Given the prevalence of divorce in Western society many children, unfortunately, will struggle with the ongoing effects of loss. It is very important to be attuned to your child's needs during this time. Communication is crucial: often, parents are so caught up in their own conflicts that they neglect the very real emotional needs of their children.

---

*I have a recurring dream about being left behind by my mother. If there is a fire, tidal wave or something that endangers our lives, someone offers to take us to safety. There is only room for one person and my mother goes with these people but leaves me behind. These dreams are depressing me and I often think about them during the day and I feel sad to think she did such a thing. What could they mean? (Rachel, 11)*

This dreamer has a heartbreaking sense of being abandoned by her mother. The worry is that it is a recurring dream, indicating an ongoing state of affairs. Not only is there a theme of abandonment, but there is a threat of a catastrophe, something overwhelming. What is happening in this girl's family? What is the nature of her relationship with her mother that she feels so clearly abandoned? She needs to be rescued, but somehow does not expect to be. It is not surprising that such dreams have given rise to a pervading depression, and I think the dreamer should have counselling as soon as possible.

*Recently I dreamed that my family was on holiday staying in a hotel. My mother and I were walking home from the movies at night and Mum was getting tired. So I carried her. I knew my way home. I was just about there when I tripped and lost my mother. I couldn't find her anywhere. I was looking behind people's doors trying to find her. I found one of my teachers in one of the houses. I didn't find my mother. (TW, 11)*

This dreamer has a heavy load to carry. He is very worried about his mother – is she ill or depressed? He mentions a teacher, an authority figure, in the dream. If he feels comfortable with this teacher I suggest he talk to him or her about the problems that he obviously has at home. He loses his mother very close to home and looks behind other people's doors. Somehow, his mother feels very elusive. He literally doesn't know where she is. She's not far, but she is lost to him. Similarly, he knows his way home, but home is a holiday hotel. Has he moved recently, or is the family in some state of flux?

Variations on the theme of getting lost or abandonment include being kidnapped and a parent or parents disappearing.

If your child has this sort of dream, it is essential to address the issues in his or her life that may be stimulating such desolate emotions. This type of dream indicates that work needs to be done to reassure the child's feeling of security in his or her waking life.

## Chased or Attacked

This very common bad dream or nightmare occurs to almost everyone. For children, it may be extremely frightening because of their perception of being much smaller. Usually, the chaser or attacker is a stranger or monster or animal (see the relevant sections in this chapter). The child may be squashed, bitten or even devoured in the dream. Generally, this dream indicates that the child feels some sort of threat is present, either in the outside world or in the inner world of their emotions. They are worried that they may be overwhelmed. The predominant feeling is dread and the necessity for self-protection.

This sort of dream is quite easy to change with time and sensitive effort on the parents' part. Suggest that your child turn and confront the attacker. Or that your daughter find a magical weapon in her flight. Or that your son call on a strong friend for aid.

## Catastrophes

This dream can take many forms: natural catastrophes such as tidal waves, floods, fire, earthquakes, storms; war; or ecological accidents. The form that children choose in their dreams depends on the emotions they are feeling and their symbolic connection to the dream event, and also the type of catastrophes they may have been exposed to in real life or through the media. Children can be affected by very graphic images.

Such themes indicate strong emotion surrounding an event or situation in the child's life. Watery dreams – flood, tidal wave, drowning, boat sinking – point to a sense of being overwhelmed and helpless. Water traditionally indicates the emotions of the dreamer, and if the water is threatening, then emotions may be in danger of breaking their containment. Water is also symbolically connected with the figure of the Mother. Ask yourselves if there is some issue in these areas with which your child is struggling.

Storm dreams can indicate a child's fear of thunder and lightning. A child may feel very small and weak in the face of a violent storm. Has your child been subjected to a storm which may have made a deep impression?

Earthquake dreams suggest that children feel something in their world is shaking apart, that the ground is unstable. This sort of dream can indicate a strong sense of insecurity about a situation.

Fire dreams have been said to indicate sexual arousal in the dreamer, although this is unlikely for children, whose sexual activity is likely to be made up mainly of curiosity and exploration rather than heat. Fire in a family home shows that the child feels that the home is under threat. Fire may also indicate a lot of anger around the child, either within or without.

War dreams are frequent in children of divorcing parents, for obvious reasons. If children feel under siege in some way – perhaps they are being bullied at school or suffer from peer group pressure or sibling persecution – war dreams may result. Boys dream of war more than girls (see Chapter 6).

Ecological disasters indicate some major threat to the child's world. Something has been ruined, or the child prefigures a sense of impending doom. There is often a lot of grief associated with these images, which sometimes mirror images that the child may have seen on television. Nuclear war is a particularly virulent threat and is worried about and often dreamed of by children. Parents can alleviate the very real fears of their children in this area by taking practical steps as a family to protect the environment, as well as discussing positive steps they can take to prevent nuclear war.

## Crashes

When children dream that they are in a car, bus, train or plane that is crashing or threatening to crash, this is a strong indication that they feel they are losing control over some elements in their life. Change may be occurring too rapidly, or they may feel at the mercy of adults who are not 'driving' the right way. Who is driving the car in the dream? Who else is on the train?

Where is the vehicle going? Elicit as many details as possible about the nature of the journey, the reasons for it, and who is travelling. These details may give you clues as to the nature of your child's worry.

---

*I had a dream where my family and I were in a car crash and I was the only survivor. My brothers were just dead but my parents were burning to death, calling my name. I was crying as well. Then I was at home wondering who I should live with and what I will do with the money from their life insurance and what bills had to be paid. Then I woke up. (Naomi, 12)*

I suspect that prior to this dream the dreamer has been involved in or overheard a discussion related to family finances and security. This dream fulfils her worst fears of being left on her own to cope with everything. The gruesome way in which her family dies may be indicative of her great fear of losing them; it is a worst-case scenario. She definitely needs to discuss this with her parents and to feel reassured. They probably need to discuss the actual arrangements that would be put in place should such a situation arise.

---

## Falling

This is a common unpleasant dream for children as well as adults. In the case of children, it may coincide with a real event such as falling out of bed, or a fall that the child has experienced in the playground or from a horse or out of a tree. A dreamer dreams of falling when he or she feels especially insecure. Ask yourselves what it is in your child's life that may have precipitated the fall. Change of any kind can evoke this image. There is also suggestion that a problem with a child's inner ear can provoke falling dreams.

## Flying

When occurring spontaneously, flying dreams are one of the most joyful that a child can experience and should be encouraged. The dream usually comes with a great feeling of freedom and power. Suggest flying as an alternative dream when any escape is required or if a child experiences falling dreams. A child who is flying in dreams should always be praised. Flying dreams usually leave the dreamer feeling light, free and happy.

## Paralysis and Suffocation

Being paralysed in the face of a terrible threat or being suffocated can be horrifying to children. These dreams may indicate an inability on the child's part to change an unbearable situation. The dreamer is trapped in circumstances in which he or she feels helpless. When a dream of this type occurs, the child may wake suddenly, gasping or thrashing about in the bed. There is some indication that paralysis and suffocation dreams may mirror the body's state during REM sleep, when the mind is active but the body is immobilised. However, if the dream recurs at all, it is imperative that parents examine the conditions surrounding their child to alleviate the feeling of entrapment that may be present (see also sexual abuse, pages 73–7).

---

*I am ten years old and I have had a dream where I am walking along a very, very skinny high bridge. My mum is forcing me to walk across it. I get to the middle but I get very scared and can't move. Please answer my dream. (Lauren, 10)*

This is a very graphic image. Quite obviously, the feeling of sheer terror and terrible insecurity is associated with the mother, although I would need to know a lot more about the family before I could assume that the mother is directly responsible for the problem behind the dream. This sort of dream is usually associated with a dramatic psychological crisis – is there abuse in the family? In this case, the dreamer may feel her mother is irresponsible for not protecting her. Perhaps the dreamer is being forced into a situation in which she feels terribly insecure through the agency of her mother: a different relationship, a different school, whatever. In any case, there is much to discuss between mother and daughter.

---

## Injury and Death

These sorts of dreams may well point to a painful emotional hurt that has been suffered by the child. Dreams of someone's death, including the dreamer's, are rarely precognitive. Death in a dream usually represents the dreamer's feeling that the person in question is causing some blockage, and the dreamer's wish that the blockage be removed. A favourite animal or toy that dies in the dream may be a mask for the child or a parent, whom the child cannot 'make die' in the dream because to do so would be emotionally too dangerous. If a child has been wounded in some way and does not want to admit it consciously, then her favourite doll or bear may die or be lost instead. Death also stands symbolically for some event or emotion having finished.

---

*I had a dream about my friend who died in a train accident. In my dream he was laughing because the train was coming. I tried to pull him off the track but the train came past and went over him and killed him. What is my dream's message? (Susan, 10)*

The dreamer is still grieving for the friend and feels somehow responsible. In the dream she tries to save him but cannot. This may be simply a way of accepting what cannot be changed, but it is important that parents discuss this dream with the child because guilt is implied, even though there is none in reality. Perhaps the dreamer had a quarrel with the friend before he died?

## Repeating Actions and Running Late

Repetition points to frustration. So if children dream that they are doing the same thing over and over again without success, or that they are too slow, or that they somehow miss the mark, frustration is the key. The dream may be quite literal: a boy may be trying to shoot goals in soccer, for example, without success. Help your child to realise his ambitions and this dream may well disappear. Similarly, dreams of running late point to frustration about an opportunity. It may be that the opportunity is missed completely, or that the child is experiencing obstacles to the achievement of a goal.

## Exams and Performance

Feeling pressured often gives rise to dreams about examinations and performance. These dreams may also include elements of the paralysis or running late variety.

Performance anxiety affects some children very deeply. It is important to let children know that they are loved whether or not they succeed at tests set for them.

## Nudity or Wrong Clothes

These dreams depict a feeling of extreme vulnerability. The dreamer feels exposed because he or she has no clothes, or because he or she wore the wrong ones. This feeling may relate to a real-life situation of embarrassment or exposure.

## Thirst or Hunger

Dreams of drinking or being thirsty usually relate to a simple physical need for moisture. Dreams of hunger, on the other hand, may relate to an emotional lack. Pay special attention to the details of such a dream.

## Good Dreams: Fulfilling Desires

While most children complain of bad dreams and nightmares, they do have pleasant dreams which show them the joyful capacities of their unconscious. These dreams remind children that they are special and that the world can hold many pleasures as well as challenges.

It is important to foster these positive dream images in your children. General discussion of dreams will encourage an atmosphere where children are inclined to remember and talk about all their dreams, not just the difficult and woeful ones. From a child's point of view, parents, if anyone, will know what to do about their dreams, especially the bad ones.

If you can develop a relationship with your children where they also bring to you their good dreams, then you will be privy to all sorts of information about their hopes and desires. It may also tell you ways in which they cope with life in general, and present you with the opportunity to nurture positive responses. These positive responses will be useful in the fight against bad dreams as well as bolstering their self-esteem for the hurdles of life.

Happy dreams will be full of the satisfaction of childish desires. Your child will receive a much-coveted present. He or she will eat table-loads of lollies and cakes. Your daughter will be a heroine and save many people; your son will be the fastest runner or swimmer or football player. He will meet movie stars and other illustrious people. She will fly planes, climb mountains and achieve the best mark in the maths exam. All of these things are possible in dreams.

Good dreams should be examined in the same way as bad dreams. Good dreams should be drawn, and role-played to reinforce the positive feeling, which will in turn encourage your child to accomplish the goals he or she has set. They may show areas of special talent, such as athletic prowess, musical ability or creative imagination. Good dreams are full of opportunities to develop a child's self-confidence. If your child dares to dream of winning, who is to say that he or she cannot succeed in waking life?

## Heroes and Superpeople

Just as the Stranger represents children's feelings of being small and helpless in the world, the hero or superperson is a projection of their desire to be in control of their own fate. They are role models for special traits of personality and powers that children want. Sometimes, the child appears as the super-person. Gradually, these fictional or mythical figures will be replaced by real-life role models, but for children, their dreams and daydreams of powerful figures are very important and should be nurtured. They balance the sense of fear in bad dreams and nightmares that children battle.

*I often have a dream where I rescue or save the life of someone. There are always other people there yet I am the one who takes over. What are these dreams telling me? (Sonya, 12)*

Does the dreamer feel as if, just occasionally, she needs to be rescued? There may be a little bit too much pressure to perform on this dreamer. Or, perhaps she needs to be given more responsibility in the family, depending on her position.

## Winners And VIPS

Children may dream of succeeding in an area that is very dear to them. These aspiration dreams are good self-motivational tools, and can provide starting points for discussion on the long process of training or practising or preparation for a goal, which is usually the stage at which children lose heart and determination. By keeping the images of the aspiration dream before them, children have a greater chance of success.

Similar to these dreams are VIP dreams, where children appear as important people, often for no particular reason. Once again, these dreams are good for self-confidence – they may in fact be compensating for a lack of confidence – but parents should point out that most VIPS only attain their status after lots of hard work and focus. Point out that they, too, will be applauded if they want to direct their resources towards that end. To parents, their child is a VIP *anyway*!

## I Want

Children sometimes dream of receiving things that they want. These wish-fulfilment dreams can reach heights of absurd fantasy, but mostly they are simple things – clothes, a new game, a pet, delicious food – that the child values and desires. This can be a difficult dream for parents, who want to give children the things that make them happy, but often do not feel that the gift is possible or even wise. You may want to discuss your reasons with your child, and perhaps come to a compromise. In the end, these dreams are pleasant ones, and much should be made of that. You could point out that, like bad dreams, good dreams don't necessarily come true!

---

*I dreamt I was wearing a long, white lacy silk dress. My hair was down to my waist. I was slim. I walked up the stairs like I was in a trance. At either side of the stairs were turrets like those of an old castle. When I got to the top there was nowhere else to go. I looked back and the wind blew my hair about. I awoke peaceful and also amazed for I am overweight, not slim. (Leanne, 11)*

This is a wish-fulfilment dream from a girl on the verge of puberty. She is a princess in the dream, going up stairs in a castle, and at the top, there is nothing else to attain. The image is of fairytale and myth. It seems the dreamer may need to keep the lovely, peaceful aspect of this image in the front of her mind. She obviously wishes to lose weight, and this is a positive dream showing her that this is possible. However, her parents should caution her that in the real world, slimness is not the most important quality for a young woman.

## Journeys and Games

Some children dream of taking special journeys and playing games that they love. Not much needs to be said here, except that parents can enjoy their children's enthusiasm, and encourage their imagination by asking them to draw or act out the dream for the pleasure of everyone in the family.

## SUMMARY

☼ Children dream thematically, but each theme or image will have particular resonance for each child, depending on their feelings about the dream.

☼ Children often have difficulty explaining dreams to their parents because of linguistic and emotional immaturity.

☼ Children remember far more bad dreams than good. Some of the common themes of bad dreams include animals, strangers, monsters, being lost or abandoned, being chased or attacked, catastrophes, crashes, falling, paralysis and suffocation, injury and death, repeating actions and running late, exams and performance, nudity or wrong clothes and thirst or hunger.

☼ Children also have good dreams, which should be encouraged. These include dreams of flying, being or meeting heroes and superpeople, being winners and VIPs, having something that they want, going on journeys or playing favourite games.

# 5

## ENCOURAGING AND INTERPRETING YOUR CHILDREN'S DREAMS

In this chapter, I suggest ways in which parents can encourage a dialogue with their children on dreams. We will also discover ways in which dreams can be constructively used by children to enhance their creativity and sense of self-worth and self-understanding.

In my book, *Wake Up to Your Dreams*, I set out a five-point plan for the recording and interpretation of dreams. I have tailored some of those methods for use with children's dreams.

One of the first issues that need to be addressed is the age of the child. As I pointed out in Chapter 1, children dream from the time they are born, and research indicates that they may have dream-like patterns in the womb. However, until a child is able to communicate in language or by drawing, it will be difficult to elicit any clear messages from your child about his or her dreams. Unfortunately, in the pre-verbal or pre-representational (drawing) phase of a child's life, there is little a parent can constructively do to encourage discussion.

If a very young child shows signs of being

distressed by dreams, then the best avenue for parents is to seek professional support. I have suggested some places you may wish to contact on page 140. A professional counsellor may be able to determine more of your child's internal state by observing the child at play, for example.

By the age of three, a child will have learned all the basic building blocks of language, and will be attempting to use that structure in speech. At around this time, children will also start to attempt representational drawing. Many parents have been thrilled but perplexed at the abstract nature of some of their child's drawings, but the industry and concentration with which most children take to pencil and paper indicates the importance of the activity!

So, in terms of keeping a dream dialogue with your child, don't expect too much structure before about the age of four. Nevertheless, the exercise itself can be a creative and useful routine to establish. A book in which toddlers can scribble their dreams before they even realise what dreams are can set up a wonderful communication, even if the words are monosyllabic and the drawings mystifying to the parent.

Children who are starting to draw quite well but cannot yet write will need you to record their dreams for them. They should be encouraged to talk about and draw out their dreams – the parent can help by perhaps writing a summary of the dream below the picture. This activity is productive: it promotes communication through speaking, drawing and writing about images that may be important to the child and which may be illuminating for the parent. Keeping the journal becomes a type of structured play time which involves the parent intimately.

At around the age of four, children will start to describe figures in their pictures. A huge scribble (which may be Daddy, for example) will gradually be replaced with a simple line drawing where a face and limbs can be made out. Children may describe a dream in a sentence such as 'the monster bit me and I ran away'. Some children at this age will be capable of drawing extremely well. They are often very concerned that details of colouring and clothing are accurate, although scale is a concept that is not usually mastered until later.

By the age of seven, much detail is apparent in the drawings. The child's language skills will almost certainly be developed enough for him or her to give you a longish description of the dream. At this point, the dream journal can be enriching for both child and parent. According to Piaget (see Chapter 2), children between the ages of five and eight start to understand the fact that dreams are internal events. It is also at this point that a more sophisticated explanation of dreams can be introduced.

Piaget suggests that lucid dreaming may occur spontaneously at this stage, but parents can introduce the concept of lucid dreaming from a very early age. It is not necessary for a child to understand the process and what it means; simple suggestion that an unpleasant dream ending can be changed will often be sufficient.

## Dream Discussions with Your Child

One of the best ways of encouraging your children to share their dreams with you is to make it a point of discussion at the breakfast table. It would help enormously if parents were to share their dreams too. Then, parents can introduce the idea of a dream journal, which will be kept by the child and discussed from time to time.

Remember that young children have trouble differentiating between fact and fantasy, inner and outer, and this will limit their ability to objectively 'interpret' dreams for themselves.

Remember also that children's dreams need to be treated with the greatest delicacy. If your child is reluctant to discuss any particular dream, do not pry unless the dream is disturbing and recurring. If you feel that your child is troubled by nightmares or bad dreams that he or she does not want to share with you, you may want to consider why. If other aspects of the child's behaviour seem troubled, then I would advise you to seek professional help.

It is most important that parents do not offer closed interpretations of dreams to children. Dreams are multi-levelled and while parents may be able to see an

Oedipal conflict being played out in the symbolism of the dream, under no circumstances should this explanation be given to the child. To begin with, many children will simply not understand the terms of the interpretation, and even if they understood, it may be very scary for them to know of such things. The parents' role is to understand and facilitate. Do not overwhelm your child with complex information that he or she may not be ready to absorb.

The point of this book and these techniques is to enlighten parents so that they can understand the problems their children will normally face, and assist them where possible. It is extremely intrusive for parents to 'interpret' their children, even if their feelings are right. Let your children come to their own conclusions. If appropriate, you can guide them in the right direction or even suggest meanings if they ask for your opinion. But under no circumstances should you impose an interpretation.

## How to Talk to Children

There are some general rules that should be used when speaking to your child, especially in relation to discussing dreams or any other part of your child's internal life.

- Remember that children must trust you not to react punitively before they take the chance of telling you something important that they feel may cause trouble. Perhaps your son needs to tell you something that he thinks you will disapprove of, or will make you cross. Perhaps his dream is about abandoning his sister or disobeying his mother. He needs to feel that he can discuss this dream without being penalised or lectured.

- Do not pressure children into talking. Provide the environment where they can feel comfortable confiding things in you, but don't force the issue. Respect their privacy and discretion.

- Don't intimidate children with ideas that are beyond them. Also, don't be a know-all. Let your child ask you the question, and answer the question that is asked without giving a dissertation on the subject. This type of response is particularly apt in the area of sexual curiosity. If your child wants an opinion, think carefully about how you couch your response. Parents may wish to stimulate the children's minds, and get them to think about all the issues involved by encouraging them to develop their own informed opinions.

For example, if your little boy is dreaming about floridly aggressive responses to danger – he shoots or stabs monsters or villains night after night – you may want to introduce the idea of discussion with the monster or villain instead of murder as a viable alternative. Perhaps you could suggest that the monster has a good side, and that it is a shame that it is always killed. Imagination is the key here. Remember that what you are doing is introducing children to a value system that you want them to follow, but you also want them to be able to think for themselves.

- Avoid analogy and metaphor with young children. They don't get it. These more adult constructions should be saved until a child has developed a more sophisticated way of thinking, at around ten years old. It is particularly important to give clear responses when a child becomes interested in things such as sex, death and God. This is not always easy, so prepare for it before the subject arises. How will you respond? Avoiding the issue altogether is equally unsatisfactory, particularly when a child is plagued by dreams in which these themes figure prominently.

- You can include fantasy, humour and the everyday in your discussions with your children. While a large part of your child's conversations with other children may seem banal and experimental, it is through playing with speech and thought that a child learns.

## The Dream Journal

Children seem to have a more vivid dream life than adults because they have not yet learned that dreams are 'silly' and best forgotten. If children are actively encouraged to discuss their dreams they will very easily develop the habit of recall.

Buy your child a big notebook full of blank pages. If your child is old enough to write, then all you need to do is mark the book up (see the following section), and let the child do the rest. I suggest you allow at least two pages to each day. Fill in the date. If your children are old enough, they will probably want to fill in these sections by themselves. If not, they may want you to – or they may simply want to scribble over the entire lot, which is fine, too!

At the end of each year, your child will have a dream journal full of dream stories and creative imagery.

The dream journal should be private if the child wants it to be, otherwise he or she may not record anything worthwhile in it. It can be a diary of the child's innermost feelings and thoughts, if that is what he or she wants. However, it is better if the journal is used as a tool for communication between parent and child, so encourage discussion whenever possible.

The child should be encouraged to fill it in as soon as possible after waking so that the memories are fresh. Make sure the journal and pencils are in the same spot each morning. The dream journal is a perfect activity for children who wake earlier than their parents.

### Filling out the dream journal

There are simple steps you can teach children to help them explain and interpret their dreams. Interpret is a big, adult word. Remember that children will comprehend the images and symbols of their dreams on a different level to you, and that you should not interpose thoughts and ideas that may confuse them. If the child is satisfied with the explanation of the dream, then that is enough. The dream has done its work for the time being.

To fill in the dream journal:

1 **Record the dream.** Write down or draw the dream in any form.
2 **Examine the dream.** This is a step that only an older child will complete. Try to separate out the major themes or elements of the dream.
3 **Write down the feelings.** This is the key to all the images and sequences. Try to establish that the feeling as it occurred in the dream is what the child should focus on. For example, if your daughter has dreamt of a huge dog barking at her, and she was able to make it friendly in the dream, but is afraid of dogs in real life, then the difference is very important.
4 **Relate the dream to the events of the day.** Is there anything about the dream that is connected to what has happened during the day? Does it

remind your child of anything else that has happened recently, or anything he or she has been thinking about?

These methods will become more complex as the child develops reasoning and language skills. Here are a few sample dream journal entries.

### The Witch Nightmare, Prue, 4

*Because of her age, Prue needed some help from her parents to fill in all the sections of the journal. She told her mother, who wrote down her dream.*

1 **Record the dream.** A witch captured my family and took them to her castle. She put them all in a big pot with water and said she would light the sticks. My grandfather was not in the pot and was very sick. I was in the room but my family didn't know I was there. The witch said I had to decide if my family got boiled or my grandfather died. She lit the sticks. I screamed that my grandfather should die and so she stopped the fire and I ran away.
2 **Examine the dream.** The witch reminded Prue of one who appears in a television programme she watches. The boiling pot reminded her of a cartoon book with cannibals who boiled their victims in a pot and then ate them. Prue was very scared of her grandfather in real life, who actually did die soon after she had this dream.

3 **Write down the feelings.** Prue felt very torn and very guilty. She found it hard to make a decision when the witch lit the sticks under the pot. She felt very guilty about deciding that her grandfather should die. She woke up from this dream crying. She also talked about how she felt about her grandfather, whom she thought was always angry with her.

4 **Relate the dream to the events of the day.** Everyone in the family was worried about the health of Prue's grandfather, who was very ill at the time of the dream. Prue was often told to stay quiet in the house, and was often left to play on her own.

It seems this dream is about Prue's unresolved feelings about her grandfather. It is important for Prue to be able to tell her parents things that may be unacceptable – that she is frightened of him, and that she resents the feeling that he is always angry with her. She may even wish that he dies so that life returns to normal. Prue's parents should spend more time with her and encourage her to express her feelings even if they are difficult.

**The Big Room, Sally, 7**
*Sally was able to fill this in mostly by herself, with her father's help in section 2.*

1 **Record the dream.** I was in a bed in a big room. There were lots of other beds lined up but no-one was in them. I was alone. The big room had windows on one side with light coming in. I looked at my hands on the sheets and they started to swell and grow huge and lumps appeared on them.

2 **Examine the dream.** There is a lot of space. Everything is big except Sally who is the smallest thing in the room. It is like the hospital corridor we visited to see Mum.

3 **Write down the feelings.** Lonely. Scared about my hands. Small. I wanted my Mum and Dad to come.

4 **Relate the dream to the events of the day.** Mum and Dad had a fight. I wish I had a brother or sister.

I would say that Sally feels very exposed and alone. Her parents have been struggling with a difficult separation, and while they were trying to hide their own problems from their daughter, she is obviously picking up the strain. The fear of her hands growing to an abnormal size may reflect a sense of self-hate that many children feel around the break-up of their parents' marriage. It may also reflect a feeling of loss of control and helplessness. The image is like something out of a horror movie, so it may indicate Sally's own horror of being left alone when her parents split up. The reference to the hospital corridor indicates her fear around this issue. Sally's mother was in hospital recently for a minor operation, but it meant that she was not around for some days. Sally's feelings of isolation may have been very acute at that time. Sally's parents need to discuss her feelings of loneliness and fear of rejection in the context of the break-up of their marriage.

**The War, Thomas, 6**
*Thomas told this dream to his father after he had drawn a picture of it.*

1 **Record the dream.** I was in a street with lots of people running. There were big planes zooming in and shooting people down. Everyone was screaming. I ran behind a building and watched. A man came up behind me with a big gun and chased me. He was trying to shoot me. I ran in all directions to get away from the bullets. I found a big rubbish bin and jumped in and hid. Then I got out and I had lost my clothes so I hid behind another building.

2 **Examine the dream.** Thomas is in a war zone. He is able to get away from the various threats that present themselves, but only just. He can hide from the dangers, but ends up with no clothes on.

3 **Write down the feelings.** Thomas feels frightened, and in the beginning of the dream, a bit excited. He is very scared when the man is chasing him and firing at him. He was shouting in his sleep. At the end of the dream, he also feels very

vulnerable, and is not only scared of the war, but also of being found without his clothes on.

4 **Relate the dream to the events of the day.** Thomas has just started at a new school which is exclusively boys. The school is much bigger than the school he was going to before. He has been quite afraid of going every morning, and is exhibiting some clingy behaviour, which is unusual. Two nights ago he watched a video with us – a Sylvester Stallone film where the hero was constantly under siege and running from danger. He was very impressed with the video and has spoken about it since.

Thomas has used the graphic images of war, gleaned from videos and television, to express his feelings of being vulnerable in a new situation. His parents need to talk to him about his concerns at school, and make sure he is not being bullied or frightened in some specific way. Hopefully, as he gets used to the new environment it will seem less like a 'war zone'. His parents probably need to monitor his television and video viewing quite carefully at present, as he is particularly susceptible to certain images, which may underscore his fears in his daily life.

## Lucid Dreaming

I have mentioned that you can teach your child to change the dream from within. This is especially useful with nightmares, when the child may feel overwhelmed by forces beyond his or her control. If the monster can be challenged, the dark stranger vanquished, the scary animal routed by the child's own actions in the dream he or she will feel a great boost to self-esteem on both conscious and unconscious levels.

The sensation of a dream within a dream is called *lucid dreaming*. For adults who may have lost the ability to recall, let alone manipulate, their own dreams, lucid dreaming can be a difficult concept. For children, lucid dreaming is usually just a matter of suggestion and practice.

Lucid dreaming has generated a great deal of controversy and the techniques can be very complex, including special methods of entering sleep, changing sleep patterns and special forms of meditation. One of the world's leading exponents of lucid dreaming, Dr Stephen La Berge, uses Tibetan yogic techniques.

Children do not seem to need the same rituals, and often spontaneously achieve lucid dreams once the concept is explained to them. In any case, complexity is likely to confuse a child. The most important step is the first: developing a sense of dream recall and developing a general awareness of dreams and dream patterns.

Rehearsal is the key. Ask your child to draw the dream and explain the characters in detail. Discuss

the possibilities: what would have happened if...?
Discuss alternative ways for the monster or stranger
or dreadful thing to behave. Discuss alternative ways
for the child to behave in the dream. If possible, play
with the ideas, literally. Give the child the monster's
role, and you take the role of the child. Then swap.
Workshop the piece. Decide on one or various
alternative endings to the dream. A joyful dream
experience can be similarly relished and prolonged.

In this way the dream becomes a sort of therapy.
Unconscious stresses and anxieties and positive
messages can be filtered through the sleeping
consciousness and be more easily integrated.

You may find that this process is enough to
prevent the dream recurring. However, if it does
recur, your child will be well armed. Depending on
the child's age and receptiveness, it may take more
than one session to cement the possibilities inherent
in lucid dreaming. This also depends on the degree
of fright the child experiences in the dream. It may
take quite a while for him or her to 'play' with this
emotion.

The underlying problem may also need to be
treated carefully. Remember that the dream is an
indicator of a certain state of affairs in the unconscious. It will not be possible to work on the dream
without unravelling the problem – if an ongoing
problem exists – at the same time. Of course, as I
have already stated, children's nightmares are

'normal', and thus may not indicate anything more than the expected fears of growing up. It is in this latter case that the techniques of lucid dreaming work most rapidly and effectively.

Lucid dreaming can also be encouraged for good dreams. If a child has enjoyed a dream, suggest that she can 'ask' for the dream to return before she goes to sleep. Or she can use elements of the dream – flight, for example – to achieve special journeys or goals. Workshop these ideas in the same way as bad dreams. This experience in a good dream can be tremendously positive for a child and will establish a skill that can be used for bad dreams and nightmares. Drawing and role-playing a good dream stimulate the imagination, and the creativity often flows on into the child's other activities.

## Night-time Rituals

Bedtime should be a warm, intimate, happy time for children. 'Bed dread' is a great creator of bad dreams and nightmares.

Predictability and routine before bed are very important. Establish a routine that suits your family and stick to it as far as possible. There may be some nights when the routine is broken, but make these nights the exceptions that prove the rule. Routine is very comforting for children, and often indicates that all is well. And if all is well, then childhood fears are less likely to press on the delicate child psyche. Monsters of the dark are less likely to intrude on sleep.

A predictable and comfortable bedroom environment is essential. Close cupboard and wardrobe doors before sleep. Draw blinds, put things back into their allotted places so that the room has its regular configuration, even in the dark.

Special time with parents is important before sleep. Children are prone to feeling very small and alone in the dark, and time spent with Mummy or Daddy before sleep can alleviate this fear. It may also be the only time in the day when a child can share intimate thoughts, feelings and fears with a parent.

A ritual for turning off the lights is a good idea. Some parents advocate prayers before hopping into bed; others have a customary cheery salute before switching off the lights.

Some children at various stages need to have a night light in their room or a light on in the hallway and the door to their room left ajar.

A bedtime story can be a good way to settle children in bed. It gives them something to think about as they fall asleep and may stimulate interesting dreams. See Chapter 6 for more on this subject.

Loneliness is a problem for some children at bedtime. One child I counselled felt her room was too far away from her parents' in a big house, and she spent the night vigilantly watching the dark for the slightest sound or noise so that she would not be attacked before she had time to run away to the parents' room. Inevitably, she fell asleep and suffered dreadful nightmares. Rearranging the rooms in the house solved the problem.

Most children form attachments to a special soft toy or blanket and it is important that this special object be present in the child's bed or at least in the room. Don't be too hasty in getting rid of these attachments. In psychological terminology they are called 'transitional objects' and are part of the child's long process of separation and the development of a sense of self. They will disappear at the appropriate stage with a little gentle prompting. Taking them away too early may generate needless anxiety.

Do not allow your child to watch violent or disturbing television programmes before bedtime. Sugary snacks can cause hyperactivity and lead to wakefulness, and some types of food such as meat, spicy food and acidic fruits before bed may be difficult to digest. It is best if the child eats at least an hour before bedtime. Milk or cheese are naturally soporific and calming as bedtime snacks.

## SUMMARY

☼ Parents should encourage a dialogue with their children on dreams. Very young children will not be able to discuss dreams, but if a young, pre-verbal child shows signs of being distressed by his or her dreams, professional advice should be sought.

☀ Although structured discussion with children about dreams is not possible before about the age of four, keeping some sort of dream journal can be a creative and constructive exercise for both parents and their children.

☀ The dream journal will develop in sophistication as the child develops linguistic and representational (drawing) skills.

☀ Parents should not offer closed interpretations of dreams to children. The parents' role is to understand and facilitate.

☀ There are skills that parents need to learn when discussing anything important with their children, including dreams. These skills include:
- not reacting punitively
- not pressuring children into talking
- not intimidating children with concepts beyond their understanding
- avoiding analogy and metaphor
- including fantasy and humour in everyday discussion.

☀ Help your child to establish a dream journal in which he or she can record and draw dreams each morning.

☀ The journal should follow a simple formula:
- recording the dream
- examining the dream and its content
- writing down the feelings associated with the dream
- relating the dream to the events of the day.

☀ Lucid dreaming is a skill that children can be taught by suggestion and practice. Lucid dreaming is changing the dream from within, and the sensation that the dreamer feels is of a dream within a dream.

☼ Bedtime rituals are extremely important to establish and will assist your child in eliminating bad dreams, and encourage good dreams.

# OTHER ISSUES THAT
# AFFECT CHILDREN'S DREAMS

## Health

The state of our health affects our dreams. Some people have been known to have dreams that warn them of current or impending health problems. Brenda Mallon states that illness is an 'archetypal or universal condition and our unconscious responds to this as it does to any other life event. Changes in the body may be noted by the unconscious before our waking brains have noticed anything at all. Indeed, such changes may be recognised in the dreams of family, friends or doctor before the "patient" has an inkling of any change' (Brenda Mallon, *Children Dreaming*, page 81).

The distinguishing characteristic of health dreams is that the dreamer awakes with the memory of a strong physical sensation, not emotion, as in other dreams. The dreams may not be bad, but they may be very persistent and the symbols may be remarkably consistent.

Do not take dreams of ill-health literally. Illness images appearing in dreams are usually symbols, just as illness itself is indicated by symbols. As we are now well aware, dream images are rarely direct, although the feelings and sensations that they impart are often very powerful.

Dreams of dying, for example, are rarely predictive. Death in dreams is a metaphor for the end of something; for example, a relationship or an emotional trauma. It can be a very positive dream. Sometimes death dreams can express a child's fear of dying, especially if they are ill at the time. Interestingly, children with terminal illnesses who know that they have a terminal illness seem to express their internal struggle and emotional reactions in highly symbolic dreams. Perhaps this is because the fact of dying is imminent – it is not just a fear, but a grim probability. Symbols are used because the full force of the realisation needs to be deflected, in typical dream-like fashion.

Carl Jung in *Man and His Symbols* describes a dream series of a ten-year-old girl that was given to him by the girl's perplexed father. The dreams were written and drawn by the girl when she was eight years old and given to her father as a Christmas present. They included symbols of a highly sophisticated archetypal nature which corresponded to very old Christian and pagan symbols which the girl could not possibly have known or understood at a conscious level. Jung studied the dreams and came to the conclusion that they indicated the girl's foreboding of her own impending death. He was correct. The child died of an infectious disease a year after giving her father the journal. In this case, the dreams were highly symbolic. Death was not prefigured directly, but through a complex interweaving of symbols of a highly archetypal nature.

Research has found that the child's concept of death varies according to age. Young children generally seem to believe that death is temporary, and involves the person being very quiet or away. At around six to eight years of age, children come to understand that death involves a cessation of normal bodily functions, but that it is mainly something that happens to older people. Only in adolescence does a truer understanding of mortality finally emerge.

Other dying dreams for children may represent a strong and violent wish-fulfilment. I have already noted that some children deal with sibling rivalry or Oedipal issues by dreaming of the death of siblings or parents. While these dreams are representative of unconscious drives designed to rid children of their source of conflict, most children will be very distressed by these dreams on awakening. It is important for parents to discuss death in a straightforward and sensitive manner, and if a conflict is indicated, to take steps to resolve the negative feelings surrounding it.

Often, the child is unconsciously attempting to make sense of death as a concept. In younger children up to around the age of seven or eight, death in dreams can often be a way of conveniently getting rid of a problematic person in their lives. As the child gets older and begins to comprehend the concept of death with more maturity, death dreams can indicate the internal conflicts surrounding the idea of mortality, both of the child and those close to him or her. These sort of dreams may be provoked by the death of a relative or friend. In this case, it is important for parents to discuss the situation with the children. Much will depend on the maturity of the child, the stability of the family and the presence – or not – of religious belief. Parents should realise that some mental experimentation with the idea of death will occur naturally in children as they grow up.

Certain physical conditions seem to provoke nightmares. Drug withdrawal following operations or illness can often lead to a surge in nightmares as REM sleep – suppressed by many drugs including alcohol and barbiturates – returns to normal. Similarly, nightmares may be experienced after long periods of disturbed sleep or extreme fatigue, as REM sleep phases rebalance. Generally, if a dreamer has been deprived of normal REM sleep for one reason or another, the period of adjustment afterwards may be marked by particularly disturbing dreams.

A child suffering fevers may complain of vivid nightmares, often filled with images of heat or fire.

Food can trigger bodily responses that result in nightmares. Children with food allergies need to be careful of their food intake, particularly before bed. Indigestion can also stimulate bad dreams. Avoid heavy, sugary or allergic foods before bedtime and try to establish a dinner routine that allows an hour or so of digestion before sleep.

The link between dreams and health has been accepted by many cultures through the ages. Indeed, until Freud started to examine the possibilities of psychoanalysis, dreams were thought to be exclusively related to the state of physical health of the dreamer. Freud noted that anxiety nightmares, culminating in a sudden, terrifying awakening, are often prevalent in dreamers with diseases of the heart while those with lung disease are prone to dreams of suffocation, crowding and fleeing.

In classical Greece, dream incubation was a commonly used healing method. Patients undertook a long purifying ritual in special temples called *asklepia*. They were given a sleeping potion and left to sleep in the sacred precinct of the temple. During their sleep, Asklepios, god of healing (after whom the temples were named), would appear and bring a healing message. The dream itself was regarded as the cure. Aristotle observed that it was highly probable that illness appeared in dreams before manifesting itself in the body because he accepted that dreams had diagnostic powers. The Hippocratic treatises state that 'accurate knowledge of the signs which occur in dreams will be very valuable for all purposes'.

Certain symbols seem to crop up frequently in dreams concerned with bodily health. If your child is dreaming of cars or houses – dream symbols of the physical body – then examine the context of the dream carefully. The car often symbolises the physical body. Who is driving the car? Is the car in control? The house represents the sense of self. Houses on fire can point to stomach problems or a fever. Is the house run down?

Bed-wetting dreams can be an expression of anxiety, like any other nightmare or bad dream. Occasional, accidental bed-wetting is a common feature of growing up, but if your child starts to wet the bed frequently and unusually there may be an underlying emotional or physical cause. Emotionally, it often indicates that changes are happening too rapidly in a child's life, and the child regresses to a stage where he or she does not have to control his or her bladder. Physically, excessive bed-wetting can be caused by bladder or urinary tract infections, worms or diabetes. Children who wet the bed report dreams of going to the toilet or of flowing water. Young children are not able to inhibit their bladders releasing in sleep, so punishment is futile. Older (above seven years) children who wet the bed may feel extremely embarrassed and shamed. Work through bed-wetting episodes with sensitivity.

Hospital visits can cause enormous fear in children. Luckily, most hospitals now are sensitive to the needs of their child patients, and parents have a greater opportunity to interact with the child in the convalescence period. Some children report bad dreams before going to hospital, and nightmares afterwards. They fear dying, the alien environment, the strange procedure that will be carried out on their body. There may also be considerable pain associated with a hospital visit. If your child experiences much anxiety and disturbed dreams as a result of a hospital visit, then dream work is advised (see Chapter 5). Patience and work should see the anxieties alleviated.

## Gender Differences and Dreams

Children's dreams are gender-specific. Boys and girls dream about different things – not exclusively, but there are themes which seem to be prevalent in boys' dreams, and others which crop up in the dreams of girls. No doubt there is much social and cultural background to sex-related differences, but it is irrefutable that gender affects the nature of the symbols in dreams from a very early age.

Freud noted that boys tend to dream of phallic symbols and girls of uterine symbols. These symbols do appear in boys' and girls' dreams at different stages of their development. Sexual difference is a fact of life, and the physical differences that go with his and hers are a source of endless curiosity to children. The nature of the symbols differ from culture to culture, but there is a disturbing preponderance of guns and weapons of destruction (phallic symbols) in the dreams of Western boys. Oddly enough, Indian boys rarely dream of such violent tools.

Girls tend to dream of events in the home. Boys tend to be more adventurous and dream of outdoor activities. Boys also dream of vehicles more frequently than girls, and the vehicles tend to be bigger and more complex. Girls dream of clothes more often than boys. Boys dream of larger animals more often than girls, whose animal dreams are often of smaller creatures such as spiders, mice and bats. As Garfield points out, 'although feminists may be initially irritated by this finding [of gender-linked differences in dreams], they may also find that dream settings can serve a unique measure to judge whether their daughters and sons are assuming the typical female and male roles or are incorporating a broader view' (Patricia Garfield, *Your Child's Dreams*, page 29).

## The Media

Childhood is a time of great change. These changes often give rise to fear and anxiety, which manifest in various ways in children's dreams. Monsters, strangers and other terrifying creatures or events embody these concerns. Linked to the issue of childhood anxiety is the issue of childhood anger and aggression.

There is one very powerful influence that actively works against the developmental resolution of childhood fear and anxiety, anger and aggression, however – the television, the omnipresent audio-visual late-twentieth-century object. Unfortunately, many television programmes promote free-floating anxiety and celebrate the visual impact of violence. For children, television monsters are truly monstrous: the Strangers in television maim, kill and kidnap; and television Witches are horribly ugly and evil.

Parents should be aware of the effects of television on their children. Some television programmes are instructive and imaginative, and should be encouraged. But there is so much on television that promotes violence, aggression and unrealistic expectations, and many of these find their way into children's dreams. I have piles and piles of letters from children where nightmare images are derived from television programmes.

---

*I recently dreamt that I was stealing items like CDs, handbags, video players with Arnold Schwarzenegger. We were in a busy city in broad daylight and people didn't seem to mind what we were doing. He was about to take a handbag from a friend's car but I screamed out, 'Don't you dare, she's my friend!' He took it anyway and I started crying hysterically.*
*(RM, 12)*

Dreaming of being accompanied by a celebrity or enjoying the company of someone rich and famous and being accepted as a friend is often a way of boosting confidence for children. It seems that the bravado of this dream backfired somewhat on the dreamer. Arnold Schwarzenegger is a movie star known for his strength. Perhaps this dreamer needs an 'alter ego' such as this because she feels weak in real life?

---

There has been continual debate on the effect of violence in the media on children. Those in favour of the censorship of violence point to their evidence; and those in favour of the free-for-all approach point out that no direct conclusions can be drawn. The latter case seems to me to be a bit like cigarette companies who deny the deleterious effects of smoking.

Advertisers and market researchers know full well the power of the transmitted image. They make millions of dollars out of manipulating the desires of their viewers, many of whom are children. Recent American research suggests that consistent exposure of children to television violence between the ages of six and eleven stimulates aggressive behaviour. Aggressive tendencies established in childhood may stunt later intellectual development and social integration. It is particularly damaging for boys, who may identify with the parade of mindlessly aggressive male 'heroes' who appear on television.

The home environment is all-important in terms of the regulation of what is and is not acceptable behaviour, but if images on television promote violence, anger and retribution every night, then the developing value system of a child can become confused. Normally, it is not acceptable for someone to resolve difficulties in their life by using stand-over tactics and aggression. It is not acceptable to kill someone because they are in the way, or in a fit of pique. Yet children are exposed constantly to television programmes that promote the unbridled use of aggression and weapons as the means to deal with the difficulties of life. On television, in the interests of drama, violent action almost always solves conflict.

---

*I am thirteen and last night I dreamt that I went to the Pizza Hut and Elle Macpherson was there. She started to sing and dance, lifting up her dress. Then she came to our table, handing out menus. I said 'hi', but when she passed our table my Mum was mean to her.*
*(Taryn, 13)*

I suspect that this young lady is projecting her growing sexuality and flirtatiousness onto Elle Macpherson. She may well feel that her mother is threatened by these developments.

---

On the evening news, children can see all the terrible cruelties that human beings are capable of committing. War, murder and disasters are dissected and served up, seemingly dispassionately, in neat sound bites. Despite the protestations of journalists and news editors the world over, the news is rarely purely objective. Once again the medium demands that the image be strong enough to compel the viewer to keep watching. From a young child's point of view, the difference between the reality of news and the fiction of violent movies is negligible.

Television encourages passivity. Children watching television are not required to interact in an imaginative way with the programmes. The dialogue, setting, colours, faces and voices are presented. There are rarely many levels of meaning. The action drives the plot and the ending resolves the action. Visual impact is the entertainment.

Horror and aggression (or 'action') are big business in the movies. To a large extent, these programmes work on the satisfaction that adults and children alike derive from projecting fears and aggressive impulses onto someone else. Jung called projections 'a bridge of illusion across which love and hate can stream off so relievingly'. Viewers passively experience the acting out of violence, aggression, cruelty (and also, happily, more positive emotions from time to time) that they cannot accept, or avoid admitting to in themselves.

The difference between adults and children in this area is great. Most adults can be objective and are able to comprehend their own projections. Children may not yet have objective skills, and will not understand how projection works. Many of these television programmes are not in the business of teaching children how to establish a strong sense of reality. So children are left to struggle with and manage their aggressive impulses and fears.

Part of the process of growing up is to experiment with these difficult but tantalising desires. For instance, being horrified is quite fun if the child feels safe. Similarly, mock battles may be thrilling; however television does not allow children to interact. It is overwhelming and graphic – heads explode, limbs are cut off, eyes pop out; victims are chased, attacked and killed; wars are fought with terrible weapons; earthquakes crumble buildings; tidal waves overwhelm; fires consume. Just like your child's nightmares.

Television is unavoidable and the positives of the medium are endless. It would be reactionary to suggest that children do not watch television. There are many worthwhile programmes that exploit the power of the medium responsibly. I suggest that parents monitor the television viewing of their children and discuss any troubling images or issues that arise.

Most particularly, avoid disturbing programmes before bedtime.

## Television Alternative: Fairytales

Bruno Bettelheim, in his book about the importance of fairytales, states:

> Most children now meet fairytales only in prettified and simplified versions which subdue their meaning and rob them of all deeper significance – versions such as those on film and TV shows, where fairytales are turned into empty-minded entertainment.
>
> Through most of man's history, a child's intellectual life, apart from immediate experiences within the family, depended on mythical and religious stories and on fairytales. This traditional literature fed the child's imagination and stimulated his fantasising. Simultaneously, since these stories answered the child's most important questions, they were a major agent of his socialisation . . .
>
> But the paramount importance of fairytales for the growing individual resides in something other than teachings about correct ways of behaving in this world . . . Fairy stories do not pretend to describe the world as it is, nor do they advise what one ought to do . . . The fairytale is therapeutic because the patient finds his own solutions, through contemplating what the story seems to imply about him and his inner conflicts at this moment in his life . . .
>
> The figures and events of fairytales also personify and illustrate inner conflicts, but they suggest ever so subtly how these conflicts may be solved, and what the next steps in the development toward a higher humanity might be. (Bruno Bettelheim, *The Uses of Enchantment*, pages 24–6.)

Fairytales can be gruesome, violent and strange. Children are lost, kidnapped, eaten; people lie, cheat, steal and kill. In that sense they are like television, but not as graphic and shallow. The action is not paramount. There is always a symbolic level to which a child's unconscious connects, and where he or she can experiment with and resolve some of the issues that dominate their lives. The fairytale is multi-levelled in a way that most television is not; it demands active imagination from the child, and it offers motifs that sustain and interest the child, even if he or she does not intellectually have any idea why.

Let's effect a comparison between two contrasting models of the archetypal hero that crop up frequently in a child's world to illustrate the difference between fairytale figures and everyday television characters.

The television hero possesses a number of classic and largely unvarying characteristics. The hero is usually male, ultimately virtuous, possesses amazing physical powers including extraordinary endurance, is able to solve any problem, usually by physical intervention (although some heroes show a fair bit of intuition), evinces clear principles of right and wrong, and he usually has a high standing in society. In this superhero world some themes are constantly replayed; for instance, male dominance, the solving of differences by violent means, the use of strong language, the predominance of weapons, a rigid structure of power and general aggression. In the end, the superhero wins out, and implicitly, his value system reigns supreme.

Things work differently in the fairytale world. The

hero is often a child, or a person in a weaker position, or someone under a spell, who overcomes mythical obstacles to achieve a life lived 'happily ever after'. Solutions are more often open-ended. Violence may be present, but is not the only way in which the protagonist overcomes problems. Often, he or she uses wit or magic, or is aided by a friendly being. Journeys, forbidden places or actions, and transformation are all fairytale elements. Bettelheim points out that in fairytale land, children can identify with fears and anxieties that they may have, and work through them with the hero to a satisfactory resolution.

## Separation, Divorce and Step-parents

One common cluster of bad dreams in children deals with the issues of separation, divorce and a new family. Today's society has seen a massive dislocation in the traditional idea of the family unit. A 1990s Australian family bear little resemblance to the classic 1950s version of two adults, three or more children, with Dad working and Mum the homemaker.

Statistics indicate that during the 1980s in Australia, 35 to 38 per cent of marriages ended in divorce. This means that around 16 per cent of Australian children can expect to deal with their parents' divorce before they reach sixteen years old.

While the breakdown in the traditional family model does not necessarily mean the breakdown of a strong value system, it does mean that children are forced to cope with change, insecurity and loss in their lives, often at critical stages of their development when security, predictability and two strong, sure parents are the ideal.

Although divorce is so prevalent in children's lives these days as to be an alternative 'norm', parents should not underestimate the effects that a family break-up can have on the children involved. Recombinant families are often viewed in terms of their lifestyle choices, a view that simply sidesteps the important emotional implications of family split-ups for the children of those families. If nothing else, the break-up of the parents interferes with the children's exploration of their sense of self in relation to gender. If the child's most intimate male authority (that is, the father) is suddenly unavailable in a constant way, it can have huge implications for the child's development. The implications of an absent father for growing boys is one of the most intensely scrutinised problems of the past years.

Another associated problem with the process of separation and divorce can be a loss of focus. Parents are often caught up in their own painful cycle of change, insecurity and loss, as well as grief, for at least some time, before life rearranges itself into a new pattern. During this period, children can find that their own normal difficulties and concerns are overlooked or trivialised. Routines can break down.

Change in family circumstances often involves a change of abode; it can also mean that parental work patterns are disrupted.

Fortunately, children are resilient and adaptable. However, most children who have experienced their parents' separation and divorce will later describe it as a defining period of their lives. Often, they are forced to accommodate emotions and actions which they do not really possess the maturity or equanimity to process.

The new family arrangement can take many forms. Step-parents and step-siblings may be involved. Children will often find themselves in blended families of various descriptions. Different access arrangements and values can exist side by side in the new family configuration. These new arrangements come complete with a new set of emotions which may be complex and conflicting. These emotions usually include the ugly attendants of resentment, jealousy and blame.

Children often report bad dreams or nightmares in the wake of a family separation. They also report a large number of wish-fulfilment dreams, where things are as they were before. Research indicates that the first two years after a divorce are critical, although children will be in a state of flux with the relationships with both parents as their normal development continues.

At a time when communication between parents often breaks down completely, it is most important that parents communicate effectively with their children. Parents need to realise that the disruption caused by separation and divorce will inevitably cause pain for a child, and that the bad dreams resulting from this pain need to be worked through constructively and openly, irrespective of how the former partners feel about each other. Issues of access, time spent with the absent parent and the feelings of loss and grief should be discussed as reasonably as possible.

One major difficulty that children encounter is the issue of truth. Who holds the truth? Who is telling the truth about the situation? It is important that parents avoid speaking too destructively about their estranged partner. If possible, a united front should be presented, in terms of explaining to children the reasons why the divorce occurred.

Children's dreams at this time may express quite naked hostility to one or both parents. Their dreams may also express guilt (many children fear that they are responsible for the breakdown of the marriage, and it is crucial that parents reassure the child to the contrary if they discover that the guilt theme is predominant), fear and insecurity (see dream themes in Chapter 4).

Step-parents and step-siblings can complicate an already difficult situation. Much depends on the age of the children to be 'blended', and their gender, and on the sensitivity and goodwill of all the adult parties involved.

Step-parents can become the focus for a child's resentment. Step-parenting is a role fraught with ambivalence, but if well handled, can make the transition to a new family arrangement much easier for a child. Some degree of mistrust should be expected at the outset. The child may complain of bad dreams in which the step-parent figures as the wicked aggressor, or as the threatening Stranger who kidnaps the absent parent or the child. Persistence, patience, clarity and consistency on the part of both the parent and step-parent will allay the fears and anxieties of the child to a great degree. Once again, it is best if hostilities and complexities are kept to a minimum. The step-parent can never replace a parent in the child's eyes, but respect and deep friendship are possible.

If your child is having disturbed dreams as a result of separation, divorce or step-parents, take the following steps:

- Discuss the dream as openly as possible.
- Ask the child what other more positive outcomes could have happened.
- Try to establish what the various figures in the dream mean to the child. Make sure you handle this one sensitively: children below the age of ten to twelve are usually unaware that they represent things in their dreams.
- Don't overreact. Remember that time and patience will solve much of the present disruption.

- Acknowledge the child's distress and hurt, and reassure him or her that they will feel better in time. Dismissing children's emotions and anger at this time will force these difficult emotions underground, where they will cause longer-term damage.
- Discuss with the step-parent strategies for dealing with your child or children, and what sort of relationship should be constructed by the step-parent with the child or children to alleviate the present stresses. Don't avoid the issue. A new family needs to be constructed as effectively as possible and leaving your child and the new step-parent to sort things out could undermine the relationship from the start.

## SUMMARY

※ Most dreams of ill-health are symbolic. However, dreams can warn of illness before the waking mind is aware of any problem. The distinguishing characteristic of health dreams is waking with the memory of a strong physical sensation.

※ Dreams of dying are disturbing but rarely predictive. They usually indicate the end of something such as a relationship or a life phase. In children's dreams they may indicate a fear of dying or a wish-fulfilment (if it is someone else who is dead).

※ Certain physical conditions seem to provoke nightmares. These include drug withdrawal, fatigue, fever and some foods.

※ Bed-wetting dreams (with bed-wetting in reality) are usually expressions of anxiety and the problem needs to be sensitively approached by parents.

☼ Hospital visits can cause enormous fear in children and bad dreams may result.

☼ Gender differences are expressed quite strongly in children's dreams.

☼ The media is a powerful influence on the images in children's dreams and parents need to closely monitor their children's television viewing habits, particularly if bad dreams are common.

☼ Fairytales are an acceptable alternative to television because they present the violent, the gruesome and the strange in mythical terms to which a child can relate symbolically.

☼ Separation, divorce and the institution of new family structures often lead to disturbing dreams in children. It is essential for parents to communicate with their children during times of family breakdown. Step-parents may become the focus for resentment and a child's anxiety in this regard should be accepted and addressed.

# CONCLUSION

Dreams are part of the mental apparatus that allows human thought and creativity to find expression. Children are born dreaming. If children's dreams are ignored or misunderstood, they may gradually lose touch with an essential element of their birthright.

Children depend on their parents to facilitate their potential. In the area of dreams, parents can do much to assist. But first, they must accept the dream is the child. By this I mean that the dream and the child are one. From the child's point of view, dreams are as much a part of his or her activity as playing, eating, loving, shouting and developing. Children know that their dreams are real, they just do not know where to put the boundaries. It is not until much later that the dream becomes a separate thing, produced by the dull adult mind as a desperate reminder of the relative nature of human experience.

If you, as a parent, help your children to understand their dreams, you are helping them to keep in touch with the most intuitive and creative part of themselves. It is this part that will help them to make the right decisions for themselves throughout their lives.

Children's dreams are the beat of their very own drum. Why muffle it? Why not help them to beat it loudly and in time with the steps they will take with growing confidence on their journey through life?

## Where to Find Professional Help

Your General Practitioner can refer you to child psychologists or psychiatrists, or try the psychology department of your local children's hospital. The Australian Psychological Society has a branch in each state.

For a list of practitioners specialising in children's problems, telephone the head office in Melbourne on (03) 9663 6166 for referrals.

# GLOSSARY

**Archetypes** Inherited, primordial images that appear in dreams and art across all individuals, cultures, languages, religions and histories. Archetypes are part of the biological apparatus of our unconscious and are activated in a child's mind by key life events.

**Compensation** One of the functions of dreams is to correct imbalances in the psychic life of the dreamer. This is referred to as the dream's compensatory function.

**Dream incubation** A technique used in the time of the classical Greeks for healing physical illnesses by sleeping in the sacred precinct of a temple. The god of healing, Asklepios, would appear to the dreamer and the dream itself was regarded as the cure.

**Dreams** Multi-layered, symbolic images created in our unconscious while we sleep to feed messages to our waking mind. Dreams express the current state of the dreamer's unconscious.

**Ego** The director of the Self. The ego balances the needs of the id and the superego through the power of reason and objectivity. The ego sets and achieves aims.

**Fairytales** A folkloric tale involving mythical figures which contains at its heart the symbolic story of a rite of passage. Children relate extremely well to fairytales because they are multi-layered, and they can identify the deeper meanings as they are ready.

**Feeling-tone**  The residual feelings that a dream leaves with the dreamer. It is important to discuss the symbols and events that occur in a dream, but the feeling-tone will be the best indication of how the dreamer is responding to those symbols and events, and thus gives a good indication of what they might mean in the context of the dream.

**Hypnagogic dreams**  Short, vivid images that occur as we are falling asleep. Sometimes accompanied by a sensation of falling.

**Id**  The inner subjective self, driven by what Freud called the pleasure principle. The id acts impulsively to achieve whatever instinctual needs are paramount at the time. A newborn mind is dominated by the id.

**Lucid dreaming**  Often described as a dream within a dream, this technique allows the dreamer to control the dream while dreaming. Children seem to dream lucidly when strong suggestions are made by parents. When lucid dreaming, a child can actively change the ending of his or her dreams.

**Night terrors**  Unlike nightmares, night terrors are not remembered by the child in the morning. A night terror usually occurs in the first half of the night, is accompanied by extreme terror, and the child may appear completely disoriented. Rarely occurring, and then most often in the two to five-year-old age group.

**Nightmares**   Dreams which are unpleasant enough to force the dreamer awake. Characterised by distressing images which are frightening for the dreamer. In children, nightmares are, to a large extent, the 'normal' accompaniments of the developmental demands of growing up.

**Oedipal conflict**   A child's unresolved desire for the parent of the opposite sex. This involves initial identification with, then later rejection of, the parent of the same sex. This is because the child comes to see the latter as a rival for the affections of the desired parent.

**Phallic symbol**   The phallus is an image denoting the erect male penis. It has come to stand for generative and destructive male power expressed through an object or image that resembles in some way the phallus. Boys will often dream of phallic symbols including guns, buildings, aeroplanes.

**Psychoanalysis**   A method first developed by Sigmund Freud to treat the underlying causes of behavioural disturbance. Psychoanalytic theory is based on the view that the conscious and unconscious thought processes are intimately related, and that revealing unconscious patterns and motivations will provide relief to conscious thought processes and personality defects such as neuroses.

**REM sleep**   Rapid Eye Movement sleep is the phase of sleep when dreams occur. Each phase of REM sleep may last up to 20 minutes, followed by periods of more or less deep sleep which last for 60 to 90-minute intervals.

**Self** The whole psyche, comprising conscious and unconscious parts, sense of inner and outer reality, and our unique and individual relationship with the people and environment surrounding us. Freud spoke of the Self in terms of three sections: the id, the ego and the superego. In a harmonious personality, all parts of the Self operate in smooth integration.

**Sibling rivalry** The jealousy that occurs quite naturally between children in the same family.

**Superego** Modulates the value system or morality of the Self, with its ideals and conscience both personal and societal.

**Symbols** Visual representations that stand for a complex group of ideas, thoughts or even people. They are imbued with meaning that is otherwise inexpressible.

**Uterine** Of the womb, or symbolically, any nurturing environment.

# BIBLIOGRAPHY

Bruno Bettelheim, *The Uses of Enchantment: The meaning and importance of fairytales*, Penguin Books, 1975, 1976.

Sigmund Freud, *The Interpretation of Dreams*, Penguin Books, 1991.

D. Bruce Gardner, *Development in Early Childhood*, Harper & Row, 1964, 1973.

Patricia Garfield, *Your Child's Dreams*, Ballantine, 1984.

Calvin S. Hall, *A Primer of Freudian Psychology*, Octagon, 1981.

Joan Hanger, *Wake Up to Your Dreams*, Penguin, 1997.

C.G. Jung, *Dreams*, Ark Paperbacks, 1985, 1986, 1989, 1991.

C.G. Jung, *Man and His Symbols*, Picador, 1978.

Brenda Mallon, *Children Dreaming: The meaning and significance of children's dreams from toddlers to adolescence*, Penguin Books, 1989.

Erich Neumann, *The Child*, Shambala, 1990.

Dr Shelley Phillips, *Relations with Children*, Kangaroo Press, 1986.

Hetty van de Rijt and Frans Plooij, *Why They Cry: Understanding child development in the first year*, Thorsons (HarperCollins), 1996.

Ruth Schmidt Neven, *Emotional Milestones*, ACER, 1996.

Phillip T. Slee, *Child, Adolescent and Family Development*, Harcourt, Brace, Jovanovich, 1993.

Anthony Stevens, *Archetypes: A Natural History of the Self*, William Morrow and Co Inc., 1982.

Anthony Stevens, *Private Myths, Dreams and Dreaming*, Penguin Books, 1995.

Anthony Storr, *The Essential Jung*, Princeton University Press, 1983.

D.W. Winnicott, *The Child, the Family and the Outside World*, Penguin Books, 1957, 1964.

# INDEX